LATIN AMERICANA RESEARCH
IN THE UNITED STATES
AND CANADA: A Guide and Directory

LATIN AMERICANA RESEARCH IN THE UNITED STATES AND CANADA: A Guide and Directory

ROBERT P. HARO

School of Library and Information Services
University of Maryland
College Park, Maryland

American Library Association
Chicago 1971

International Standard Book Number 0-8389-0093-3 (1971)

Library of Congress Catalog Card Number 72-138653

Copyright © 1971 by the American Library Association

Printed in the United States of America

To our son Richie

CONTENTS

PREFACE

Latin America has long been an area of on-again, off-again interest for North Americans. Because of its proximity to the United States, strong economic and military ties are evident and perhaps necessary. As of this date, sociopolitical relationships between this country and the various Latin American republics range from casual relations to belligerent concern and suspicion. In spite of these conditions, too little research and study dealing with this vast area have been undertaken by North Americans. As a result, Latin America is relatively unknown to most of us aside from the many stereotypes frequently employed by newspaper cartoonists on the editorial pages of American dailies. The news media have also been lax in their coverage of this geographical area, reporting news only when it concerns a major natural disaster, a revolution, or a coup d'état. In addition, our government officials have tended to consider the other American republics lightly, regarding them seriously only when they presented this country with some form of crisis which could not be avoided.

The advent of a Communist government in Cuba and the marginal results of the Alliance for Progress indicate that we cannot remain ignorant of the republics to the south of us. With this in mind, the present directory has been prepared to assist students, scholars, researchers, librarians, and informed laymen in their investigations on this vast region generally referred to as Latin America.

A goodly number of bibliographies exist devoted to one or more countries and subjects in Latin America. But who has what collection of library materials and information resources? Who is conducting ongoing research on one or more countries or subjects from Latin America? What major tools are available to help the serious student, scholar, librarian, or informed layman identify important materials located close to him? How does a librarian start or develop a good working collection of Latin Americana? These are some of the questions that this guide should answer.

A few remarks are in order concerning the sources of data here presented. A preliminary questionnaire was drawn up and circulated to a few Latin American specialists as a pretest. After some modifications resulting from the remarks and suggestions of these specialists, a final version was completed. Approximately 200 questionnaires were then sent out, and much to the compiler's surprise 135 were completed and returned, representing a 68 percent return. In addition, the compiler visited many of the libraries and research centers personally. For those institutions that failed to respond to the questionnaire, it was necessary to rely upon information from secondary sources. A few libraries and research centers whose data on their collections and operations were insufficient were not included in this compilation. It is to be hoped that in a future revision and updating of this directory new organizations and established libraries and research centers not here included will provide data and information on themselves.

The guide is divided into three parts. The first part, the Introduction, discusses the Farmington Plan (a cooperative book-gathering plan); the Seminar on the Acquisition of Latin American Library Materials; the Latin American Cooperative Acquisitions Program; and important printed book catalogs in the field. The second part lists and briefly describes the countries and subject strengths represented in the collections of established or developing Latin American library collections in the United States and Canada. The third part lists research centers that have continuing programs of research and investigation dealing with one or more aspects of Latin America. In both the second and the third parts, the listings of libraries or research units include the address, telephone number(s), director(s), library specialist(s), staff member(s) engaged in developing the Latin American collection, size, brief description of the collection (including special collections and subject strengths), and additional pertinent information. An Addenda lists institutions whose data were compiled, not from questionnaires or personal visit, but from secondary sources. There are three indexes: country, Latin American library specialists, and subject. The numbers in the index sections refer to the numerical listings of the organizations in the directory, not to page numbers.

It is with the warmest affection that I express my thanks to my wife for her patience and encouragement throughout the three years in which I worked on this project. At times I would abandon her and our children either to assume a monastic existence, or to travel to a distant library or research center for needed information. Her forbearance and understanding were truly magnificent. I also wish to extend my most sincere appreciation for the assistance of Mrs. Gayle Araghi in helping me to prepare the indexes and in proofreading the first section.

Information for this guide has a cutoff date of June 1969. The responsibility for any errors of fact or interpretation rests, of course, entirely with the compiler. Constructive comments and suggestions for ways of improving the guide are earnestly solicited in anticipation of a following second edition.

ROBERT P. HARO

School of Library and Information Services
University of Maryland
College Park, Maryland

INTRODUCTION

A number of institutions, programs, and other aids, such as printed book catalogs, have served to nurture the growth of Latin American research collections in the United States and Canada. A discussion of some of the more important of these is given below.

THE FARMINGTON PLAN

The first stirrings of what was later to become the Farmington Plan began in 1939. The then new Librarian of Congress, Archibald MacLeish, realizing that the outbreak of war in Europe meant that American scholars would be denied access to many of the most important European collections of research materials, called upon librarians and scholars for advice in meeting the crisis. The first formal use of the name occurred in October of 1942 when the Executive Committee of the Librarian's Council of the Library of Congress held its third meeting in Farmington, Connecticut. In 1947, the Association of Research Libraries formally adopted the Farmington Plan as its own, and in 1948 the first stage of actual operation was implemented with the decision systematically to acquire publications issued in France, Sweden, and Switzerland during that year. Subsequently, the plan was greatly expanded geographically so that now it is virtually worldwide in coverage.

The Farmington Plan, in essence, is a voluntary agreement under which more than sixty American libraries have accepted special responsibility for collecting foreign published materials as a means of increasing the nation's total resources for research. The plan's primary goal is to place at least one copy, in an American library, of each new foreign publication that might reasonably be expected to interest the research worker in the United States. Each participating library is responsible for the publications of one or more geographical areas of the world and is required to list promptly in the *National Union Catalog,* and make available by interlibrary loan or photographic reproduction, all materials acquired from such areas.

Two important patterns of acquisition under the Farmington Plan require differentiation: subject responsibility and country responsibility. The pattern of *subject responsibility,* which has been the basis for allocation of the publications of Western European nations and a few others, requires that a dealer in each country, chosen by the responsible library, obtain a copy of each new book published in his country that falls within the scope of a carefully defined subject area and send it to the library responsible for the subject it treats. Unfortunately, this system of dealer-academic library relations has not been successful in Latin America, primarily for the reason that the book trade in these countries is very poorly organized. As of this time, only the larger research libraries have been able to engage, and with only very limited success, in such ventures.

Of much greater importance for the systematic acquisition of books published in Latin America is the pattern of *country responsibility,* according to which a single library takes responsibility for all publications of a country and makes its own arrangements for acquisition. The development of area studies programs, such as the Caribbean, Central America, Cuba, and so on, within academic institutions has encouraged some of the libraries of such institutions to undertake responsibilities of this kind.

The administration of the Farmington Plan is under the jurisdiction of the Association of Research Libraries, which, for the most part, comprises the participating institutions. These include the country's largest university libraries and other major research collections, such as the Library of Congress, the New York Public Library, and the John Crerar Library. Not all members of the Association participate in the plan, however, and several nonmembers have accepted acquisition responsibilities under it. Notwithstanding these exceptions, all questions of policy are decided by a vote of the Association, which formally meets twice a year. More precise information on the Farmington Plan is available in Edwin E. Williams's book, *Farmington Plan Handbook,* Washington, D.C., Association of Research Libraries, 1961.

Following is a list of the Latin American countries and the libraries responsible for the systematic acquisition of their materials:

COUNTRIES AND RESPONSIBLE LIBRARIES

ARGENTINA	Syracuse University Libraries
BAHAMA ISLANDS	University of Florida Library
BARBADOS	University of Florida Library
BOLIVIA	Duke University Library
BRAZIL	University of Illinois Library
BRITISH GUIANA	University of Florida Library
BRITISH HONDURAS	University of Florida Library
CHILE	University of California, Main Library, Berkeley
COLOMBIA	University of Arizona Library
COSTA RICA	University of Kansas Library
CUBA	University of Florida Library
DOMINICAN REPUBLIC	University of Florida Library
ECUADOR	Duke University Library
EL SALVADOR	Tulane University Library
FRENCH GUIANA	University of Florida Library
GUADELOUPE	University of Florida Library
GUATEMALA	Tulane University Library

HAITI	University of Florida Library
HONDURAS	Tulane University Library
JAMAICA	University of Florida Library
LEEWARD ISLANDS	University of Florida Library
MARTINIQUE	University of Florida Library
MEXICO	University of Texas Library, Austin
NETHERLANDS ANTILLES	University of Florida Library
NICARAGUA	Tulane University Library
PANAMA	University of Arizona Library
PARAGUAY	Syracuse University Libraries
PERU	Cornell University Library
SURINAM	University of Florida Library
TRINIDAD AND TOBAGO	University of Florida Library
URUGUAY	Syracuse University Libraries
VENEZUELA	University of Virginia Library
WEST INDIES FEDERATION	University of Florida Library
WINDWARD ISLANDS	University of Florida Library

For the convenience of the reader the above list of "Countries and Responsible Libraries" is given in reverse order below as "Responsible Libraries and Countries":

RESPONSIBLE LIBRARIES AND COUNTRIES

Arizona. University	COLOMBIA
	PANAMA
California. University. Main Library. Berkeley	CHILE
Cornell University	PERU
Duke University	BOLIVIA
	ECUADOR

Florida. University	BAHAMA ISLANDS
	BARBADOS
	BRITISH GUIANA
	BRITISH HONDURAS
	CUBA
	DOMINICAN REPUBLIC
	FRENCH GUIANA
	GUADELOUPE
	HAITI
	JAMAICA
	LEEWARD ISLANDS
	MARTINIQUE
	NETHERLANDS ANTILLES
	SURINAM
	TRINIDAD AND TOBAGO
	WEST INDIES FEDERATION
	WINDWARD ISLANDS
Illinois. University	BRAZIL
Kansas. University	COSTA RICA
Syracuse University	ARGENTINA
	PARAGUAY
	URUGUAY
Texas. University. Austin	MEXICO
Tulane University	EL SALVADOR
	GUATEMALA
	HONDURAS
	NICARAGUA
Virginia. University	VENEZUELA

SEMINAR ON THE ACQUISITION OF LATIN AMERICAN LIBRARY MATERIALS

The first Seminar on the Acquisition of Latin American Library Materials (SALALM) was held in 1956 to encourage the acquisition and control of Latin American materials in the United States. A representative group of librarians and bookmen was invited by the Pan American Union and the University of Florida "to consider the problems involved in finding, buying, and controlling library materials related to Latin America." Specifically these problems fell into three categories:

1. How to know what has been and is being issued

2. How to get what is needed for the particular library

3. How to process and preserve the material acquired.

The seminar, then, had its inception in a meeting of concerned librarians, bookmen, and specialists convened to consider these three problems. Various papers were presented at the first meeting, more as position papers requesting action on issues rather than as final papers proposing solutions. It was decided, toward the end of the first seminar, to hold a second one the following year.

By the time of the second seminar, modest funding had been provided by the Council of the Organization of American States for an expanded library development program in the Pan American Union, and the Rockefeller Foundation had made available funds to create an Inter-American Library School at the University of Antioquía in Medellín, Colombia, mainly as the result of needs cited during the first seminar. From 1957 through 1959, the now annual seminars were bringing together a number of important librarians, bibliographers, and specialists. In addition, major academic and research libraries consistently sent representatives to share their knowledge and experiences and to gain new insights.

The initial structure of the seminar was quite flexible. Ad hoc committees were constituted to consider major problem areas as they were perceived by the group. Leadership within the seminar rapidly fell to those individuals representing major institutions with sizable collections of Latin Americana. A continuing membership gradually developed within the loosely constituted organizational structure. Each annual seminar was initiated by a particular group of members who planned not only the working sessions, but also arranged for the site, the speakers, and the topics to be covered. In the meantime, many of the issues raised by the seminars were thoroughly investigated during the year by both persons and institutions. This unceasing activity resulted in the establishment of important library programs and projects, a good example of which was the development of fruitful, ongoing relations with reliable bookdealers in Latin America.

Gradually, the seminar came of age. At the thirteenth seminar held at the University of Kansas, SALALM became incorporated as a membership association of an educational character. No immediate changes in the basic organizational structure of the seminar resulted. Incorporation permitted a gradual conversion to a more flexible organization than that available under the loosely structured system employed by the older seminars. As gradual changes occurred, new permanent standing committees were created: (1) Constitution and Bylaws, (2) Policy and Research, (3) an Editorial Board, and (4) an Advisory Committee to LACAP (Latin American Cooperative Acquisitions Program).

The formal organization of SALALM as an educational association allowed it to apply for tax-exempt and tax-deductible status in the United States, with the result that it now seeks grants and carries out specific projects of interest to its membership.

To accomplish its purposes, each year SALALM identifies a variety of problem areas for investigation. Several ongoing projects, such as the cooperative cataloging project involving the Library of Congress, were the subject of extensive research and investigation carried over from year to year. The seminar annually invites specialists to organize or expand upon knowl-

7

edge dealing with pertinent topics and issues. These reports may take the form of working papers, ranging from the fields of subject strengths of existing Latin American collections at American colleges and universities to brief guides for purchasing retrospective materials and block collections from Latin America. Usually, these position papers make available the experiences and expertise of authorities to any librarian interested in developing a collection of Latin Americana or solving associated· problems.

Along with the identification of materials, the seminar has been very active in establishing close ties with bookdealers and agents in Latin American countries, as demonstrated by the Latin American Cooperative Acquisitions Program to be discussed in more detail on page 12. The acquisition and organization of Latin American materials by smaller libraries have been of considerable concern to the seminar. At the time LACAP was initiated, other programs addressing themselves to the specific problems of smaller libraries were undertaken. Some of these projects included the United States Book Exchange, the Public Law 480 Program, cooperative cataloging agreements, and guides for the identification of government publications of the various American republics, including descriptions of important series and ways of securing them.

The activities of the seminar may perhaps be best described as applied research. Its publications provide a wealth of pertinent data and information that librarians and specialists can apply to the resolution of their own problems. Furthermore, this information is as germane to the small library as it is to the larger research and specialized libraries. In fact, the cooperation between theoretically oriented academicians and the practical bookman, between librarians in the United States and Canada and their counterparts in Latin America, and between all levels of library specialists in the Americas is a truly remarkable achievement of SALALM.

There are, however, some serious weaknesses of SALALM

that must be presented. To the perceptive specialist and the informed layman, the list of participants at the annual seminars must appear as a round robin tournament. The same faces representing the larger institutions seem to form a closed leadership that only grudgingly accepts newcomers. While the newcomers may be tolerated as participants, they are carefully restricted from holding substantive leadership roles within the seminar. Perhaps this condition is a carry-over from the practice in other library associations, where administrators tend to form leadership cliques that exclude even specialists from the governing and directive functions. Also, the attitude of many administrators from larger and more prestigious libraries is that of being "worthier than thou," especially when dealing with colleagues from smaller libraries or the occasional scholar-participant.

Lack of funds may be a problem prohibiting many talented and concerned librarians and specialists from either regular or occasional participation at the annual seminars. An attempt to remedy this situation by holding the annual meetings at different sites throughout the country has both advantages and disadvantages. An even greater problem involving finances is the necessity for not only participants, but contributors and speakers as well, to pay their own way to the annual meetings. It is not remarkable, therefore, that only the larger and wealthier libraries and institutions across the country seem to be consistently represented. Perhaps under the new organizational structure, the seminars will be characterized by broader representation, and through the judicious use of funds attract more of the younger, talented librarians capable of significant contribution but heretofore lacking financial assistance for travel.

Concerning the seminar *Proceedings* themselves, one can only be amazed at the cavalier attitude shown in editing and publishing them. The final reports and working papers are poorly organized and printed, and suffer from pedestrian advertisement and publicity. The form in which they have been issued effectively prevents any systematic use of the various volumes. In addition, the format for each volume is poor and highly disorganized, to say the least. While the contents of the working papers and reports are of tremendous value, the lack of adequate indexing of even title and author listings, or of some form of cumulated table of contents for the previously issued works, is almost appalling. Here, then, are significant pieces of research, scholarship, and expert advice needed by present and perhaps future librarians and specialists, lost for all practical purposes. The emphasis on bibliographic control and the organization of knowledge that the seminar has recognized as needed on Latin American library materials seems to have escaped the body in its treatment and arrangement of its own thoughts, research, insights, and advice.

While not an act of commission, but certainly one of omission, a conspicuous failure is the absence of critical surveys devoted to book-gathering plans, the organization of library materials, and the cooperation of American libraries in sharing their resources. To date, there are few if any statistical surveys of interlibrary loans dealing with Latin American materials. The accounts of LACAP and other book-gathering plans for Latin America are highly praiseworthy; the weaknesses—and they do exist—seem never to be articulated. Furthermore, the insufficient data in American libraries concerning new acquisitions, reprints, out-of-print titles, average costs, processing costs, preservation of paper, binding problems, and the items most frequently sent on interlibrary loan present another of the problem areas that require serious investigation, quantification, and interpretation by appropriate specialists. Nor are concepts of regional cooperation among American libraries discussed critically and realistically during the seminar meetings. The great metropolitan centers of the United States—Boston, Chicago, Detroit, Los Angeles, New York, Philadelphia, Saint Louis, San Francisco, and Washington, D.C.—have not been considered as focal points for cooperation among libraries seeking to make available necessary materials for the serious student, the scholar, and the informed layman. It may well be that many libraries with rich Latin American collections are quite prepared to discuss their strengths and weaknesses, but are chauvinistic about cooperative lending and service programs.

It is at this point that a serious weakness within the seminars may tend to override its many accomplishments. That weakness is the limited approach toward the dissemination and use of library materials that has characterized the attitude of seminar participants. The annual meetings devote considerable time to issues related to the securing and handling of traditional materials. Yet two very important problems are never completely pursued. First, nonbook materials, with the exception of government publications, receive only sporadic and pedestrian review. Secondly, the seminars seem to have focused their attention on securing and organizing materials with little if any regard to serving the needs of researchers, scholars, and students. Librarians in charge of Latin American library collections are in danger of becoming custodians of these materials rather than experts in their dissemination. It is obvious that a critic of SALALM can easily prepare a list of reservations bearing on the goals and concerns of the annual seminars. Important as the meetings have been, they have, nonetheless, tended to neglect certain vital areas, among which are the determination and identification of the needs of researchers and scholars; the amalgamation of a variety of materials and resources in the teaching and research programs; the preparation of studies addressed to the topic of how best to employ Latin American library specialists; the proper training and preparation of Latin American specialists; the formulation of library school curricula designed to educate the future Latin American specialists; and consideration of the modification of severely restrictive interlibrary loan codes which frequently now inhibit the fullest possible dissemination of Latin American materials. These are some of the problem areas which it is hoped SALALM will consider in future meetings.

The work of the seminar has filled a tremendous gap, but SALALM's success thus far only foreshadows its potential for achievement. If it presses its investigations of those neglected problem areas listed above as vigorously as it has those problems with which it was initially concerned, SALALM's promise for the future is great indeed.

LATIN AMERICAN COOPERATIVE ACQUISITIONS PROGRAM

Discussion of the Seminar on the Acquisition of Latin American Library Materials is incomplete without a description and review of the Stechert-Hafner Corporation's Latin American Cooperative Acquisitions Program. LACAP, as it is popularly called, originated as a result of the seminar, and it was, to a great extent, a manifestation of a larger trend toward cooperative acquisitions programs and projects sweeping across the United States and Canada. Earlier in this section, the ambitious Farmington Plan was described, particularly as it relates to and affects Latin American library materials. While the Farmington Plan is an academically oriented cooperative agreement among research libraries in the United States and Canada, LACAP is a cooperative, commercial enterprise.

The Latin American Cooperative Acquisitions Program was organized in 1960 as a result of the deliberations and recommendations of SALALM. More than four years of preliminary discussions and six months of intensive planning occurred in advance of LACAP's official organization. Following the fourth seminar in Washington, D.C. (1959), several participants gathered informally. The conversation gradually focused on a discussion about establishing a traveling acquisitions agent in Latin America. The issues that had prompted agreement on the need for a traveling agent were: the difficulties of obtaining library materials from Latin America before they went out of print; identification problems caused by the lack of description,

12

advertisement, or publicity of titles published by small and private presses; and the general disorganization of the Latin American book trade. The consensus was that a traveling agent or agents in Latin America, sponsored by private enterprise encouraged by the profit motive, offered a possible, permanent avenue to the effective acquisition of Latin American library materials. As the assistant vice-president of Stechert-Hafner was present, the inevitable question asked by the group was, "Why doesn't Stechert-Hafner do it?" Intrigued with the possibilities and encouraged by the support of SALALM members and participants, Stechert-Hafner approved the project for implementation with the requirement that it should break even financially within three years.

A highly qualified purchasing agent was selected to begin extensive traveling in Latin America to identify the bookdealers and other reliable sources of library materials in each country or distinct geographical area. Originally there were only five participants in the venture, counting Stechert-Hafner. But before the end of January 1960, the United States National Agricultural Library joined the plan. Cornell University and the University of Southern California became members in February of that year. While LACAP was not self-supporting by the end of 1960, the picture began to change considerably, and by the end of 1961 the program was meeting its cost.

As LACAP approached the end of its proving period in June 1962, it was well on its way to becoming self-supporting. There were significant expansions in the coverage of the plan, and a permanent agent for operations in Latin America was employed. Also, the New York office of Stechert-Hafner improved its administrative control and hence increased the quality of the program. Participation in the plan increased and began to extend beyond the United States. By the end of 1962, LACAP, for all practical purposes, was a financial success.

American libraries now had a reliable purchasing system for the procurement of Latin American library materials, the success of which was demonstrative of the broader achievements of SALALM. Through a technique which consists essentially in search and supervision by a traveling agent, the participating libraries have received almost 25,000 current titles. In addition, more than 18,000 retrospective titles have been made available to participating libraries. The purchase of new titles by Latin American authors before they go out of print has enabled libraries to develop well-balanced Latin American collections. The geographical coverage is perhaps the most complete ever achieved. Not only are all the major Latin American countries covered, including those in Central America and the Caribbean, but the publications of the provinces share the same coverage as those of the capitals. As of this date, Cuba remains the only Latin American country not included in the plan. However, Cuban publications are available through and from other Latin American countries.

But enough about LACAP's background and success; how does it work? The purpose of LACAP as a cooperative enterprise is to provide participants with a steady flow of printed materials currently published in all the countries of Latin America. To participate in LACAP, a library need only place a general order for new materials to be supplied on a continuous basis as they arrive. Such an arrangement may be tailored to the specific needs of the library and can be restricted to the publications of particular countries as well as to specific subject areas. There are no charges other than the cost of the books themselves. At present more than thirty-five libraries participate in LACAP. Current published books in all subject fields by Latin American authors from all the Latin American countries presently average about 5,000 titles a year at a cost of approximately $20,000. These figures, of course, represent the *maximum* number of titles that can be received and the *maximum* cost involved. Stechert-Hafner will provide estimates of the annual participation costs for publications from specific countries, or within specific subject areas.

In addition to limiting the scope of the plan to particular countries or specific subject areas, there are other special restrictions that a library may request of Stechert-Hafner. These include the following:

books by Latin American authors and published by publishers in their country be sent only

new editions or reissues be sent only when they are augmented or corrected, i.e., with new prefaces, new introductions, or critical new material

no juvenile literature, textbooks, translations, or academic theses or dissertations be sent

no separate volumes from a series whose first number appeared before 1960 be sent

only the first issue of a new serial be sent

no books costing more than $25 net be sent before confirmation, and

no books less than fifty pages in length be sent.

In addition to limiting the scope of the plan for interested libraries, LACAP allows anyone to order publications from its catalogs. However, items ordered from the catalogs may often be sold before the orders are received and additional copies from abroad may be difficult, if not impossible, to secure.

The primary advantage of participation in the plan is that LACAP provides a blanket order approach to Latin American materials. As with other blanket order and gathering plans, participating institutions are assured of delivery as soon as possible after publication. They are able to maintain systematic coverage with a minimum of expertise and cost. Not only do they learn of books before they are recorded in any bibliography, but they receive the books themselves. Since they need retain only those items appropriate to their collections, participating libraries can avoid an infusion of publications of no value to them. A second basic advantage of the blanket order procedure is that it affords libraries and librarians a broad overview of what is being published in given subjects, from particular countries, and by specific writers. Furthermore, librarians evaluating new arrivals on the LACAP agreement gradually attain a sharpened awareness of Latin American writers, literature, and trends. A final, and perhaps more subtle, advantage to participation in LACAP is the almost all-inclusive nature of it and the good will that it generates among researchers, scholars, and students toward the library.

It would be a disservice, however, not to present some of the weaknesses of LACAP. First, there is the question of its suitability to various types of libraries. It must be stated that the plan works most effectively for the relatively affluent institution which can participate fully. Smaller institutions, by virtue of financial exigencies, must limit themselves by employing some or all of the authorized restrictions specified above. Such limited participation often results in an unsatisfactorily diluted coverage of Latin America. Another factor which weighs against small institutions deriving the maximum possible benefit from the plan is that participation frequently requires additional support staff in an order department and may also entail additional correspondence, routines, and practices.

Experience has indicated that subject coverage available under the plan is uneven, e.g., materials in the sciences, and particularly the biological sciences, are inadequately represented. Again, collective experience with the plan discloses that the quality of materials available is uneven. Hence, a participating library, in order to gain maximum advantage from the plan, must employ the talents of a person familiar with Latin Americana to function as a selector. Furthermore, the selector should have a detailed knowledge of his library's plans for developing its collections in Latin Americana, its available resources, and the supporting university's curricula.

16

Many of the larger academic libraries, once LACAP participants, have dropped their membership. They have done so because of their development of their own arrangements and devices for procuring necessary library materials. A few smaller libraries, feeling the pressure of inflation and slowly declining increases in book funds, have similarly dropped their membership. Competition from rival plans that cater more to developing academic libraries has also caused many libraries to question continuing membership in LACAP.

Of a more serious nature is the steadily increasing orientation of LACAP toward the larger academic and research libraries of the United States and Canada. Probably it is the commercial nature of the enterprise that requires Stechert-Hafner to tailor its program to the needs and resources of high-volume subscribers. Be that as it may, many smaller libraries are still looking for a procedure that will enable them to develop or initiate Latin American collections. Until a smaller and less ambitious program is available, the larger institutions will continue to be the ones that will profit from the full potential of LACAP.

Although the above weaknesses in LACAP do exist, its value is unprecedented in the field of commercial, cooperative acquisition ventures. Prior to its inception, nothing of such ambition and magnitude was available. The future of Latin American collection development within American libraries will definitely hinge upon how well LACAP fulfills its purposes and how responsive it is to all libraries, not just to participating members. On the basis of past experience, that future is bright indeed. For a more detailed account of the history and beginnings of the Latin American Cooperative Acquisitions Program the reader should refer to M. Jennifer Savary's book, *The Latin American Cooperative Acquisitions Program . . . an imaginative venture*, New York, Hafner Publishing Co., 1968. Although essentially a glowing account of the history and development of the program, it contains important statistical comparisons, tables, and pertinent information that should be of considerable interest and value to librarians interested in the costs and results of participation in the LACAP plan.

PRINTED BOOK CATALOGS

Several American libraries owning outstanding collections of Latin Americana have arranged through the offices of G. K. Hall & Co., Boston, Mass., to have their card catalogs published in printed form. This section lists and describes all such printed catalogs, copies of which are to be found in most of the major research libraries in the United States.

Recourse to a printed dictionary catalog will quickly disclose to the serious student the full scope and breadth of the library's holdings on a particular subject of interest to him. The other basic use of the catalogs is to reveal immediately whether the library whose printed catalog is being consulted owns the particular item. Upon discovering that it does, the student can then arrange to secure it through interlibrary loan. Librarians, bibliographers, and bibliophiles find other uses for these catalogs: as selection, verification, and ordering guides; as locating devices for securing scarce materials; and as sources of comparative data on variant editions and printings. Because the rules of entry governing the compilation of these catalogs vary, the student is advised to examine carefully each catalog's introductory material in order to use the listing to maximum effectiveness.

The catalogs, as briefly described below, indicate the date of the work, usually the number of cards or entries contained, and descriptive details on the nature and scope of the collection:

Boston Public Library. *Catalog of the Spanish Library, and of the Portuguese books bequeathed by George Ticknor.* Boston: G. K. Hall, 1970.

Originally published in 1879, this work describes what still is an outstanding collection of Spanish literature. It is very useful as a bibliographical tool for the scholar, as it not only records those works which comprised George Ticknor's library, but also includes analytical references to works in larger collections and in serial publications. An appendix lists in short-title form those books and manuscripts which fall within the scope of the original catalog that have been acquired since 1879. The works have been separated into more specialized categories better to represent current interest, such as Spanish, Portuguese, and Latin American sections.

California. University. Berkeley. Bancroft Library. *Catalog of printed books*. Boston: G. K. Hall, 1964. 22v.; Suppl., 6v.

The Bancroft Library is a unique library that concerns itself with the area from Alaska to Panama and from the Montana-Texas line westward to Hawaii and the Pacific Islands, with particular emphasis on California and Mexico. The collection is strongest in the social sciences, particularly history, religion, politics, economics, and social conditions. Special strengths include publications by and about the Catholic church in Mexico; early California printing; voyages and travels; official government publications of New Spain; and the pioneer west.

California. University. Berkeley. Bancroft Library. *Index to printed maps*. Boston: G. K. Hall, 1964.

Some 10,900 cards comprise this catalog of maps in the Bancroft collection. These maps are of the New World, with emphasis on the western half of North America, including Mexico. The maps date from the 16th to the 20th centuries and are classified according to an adaptation of the Library of Congress system, supplemented by added and subject entries filed by area or special interest, such as land grants or roads and land routes. Among the various types of maps indexed are geological, ethnological, and linguistic maps of areas and regions. The older maps, showing locations of trails, battlefields, Indian tribes, ranches, missions, mines, expedition routes, and so on, are unique sources of information.

California. University. Los Angeles. Research Library. *Dictionary catalog*. Boston: G. K. Hall, 1963. 129v.; 2,703,-000 cards.

The UCLA Library maintains various collections of materials to service interdisciplinary institutes of research and teaching, among which is the Latin American Studies Center. In addition, the library has significant holdings in history, political science, literature, and sociology as it relates to Latin America. The catalog is a dictionary type with all entries, whether by author, title, subject, or series, being in one convenient alphabet.

Canal Zone Library-Museum. *Subject catalog of the special Panama collection*. Boston: G. K. Hall, 1964.

This collection contains some 5,000 books, reports, drawings, maps, diaries, photographs, clippings, newspapers, and magazines. The library collection pertains to pioneer exploration and voyages in the region; early surveys for a canal and a railroad; and post-1914 projects for improvement of the canal and for a sea-level waterway. The catalog cards are arranged alphabetically under approximately 500 Library of Congress subject headings.

Catholic University of America. *Catalog of the Oliveira Lima Library*. Boston: G. K. Hall, 1970. 2v.; 34,700 cards.

The principal focus of this catalog is the Luso-Brazilian world. It comprises the collection of Oliveira Lima, well-known historian and Latin American scholar. Since the collection was donated to the Catholic University in 1916, it has continued to expand substantially until it is now considered one of the foremost in the world in the areas of Portuguese and Brazilian history and literature.

In addition to important source material on Portuguese colonial expansion and the history of Portugal, this dictionary catalog is a rich source of material on the events shaping Brazil's destiny from its earliest contacts with Portuguese civilization and on the literary outpouring produced by its turbulent growth.

Harvard University Libraries. *Latin America and Latin*

American periodicals. Cambridge: Harvard University Library, 1966. 2v.

A very important work that lists ca. 30,000 titles, being primarily works on history, civilization, government, general geography and travel, general economic and social conditions, religious affairs, and the various races of the West Indies, Mexico, and Central and South America. Volume 1 includes a classification schedule and a classified listing by call number. Volume 2 includes an alphabetical listing by author or title and a chronological listing by date of publication.

Hispanic Society of America. *Catalogue of the Library.* Boston: G. K. Hall, 1962. 10v.; 211,000 cards.

This very important collection in New York City contains more than 100,000 volumes covering the cultures of Spain, Portugal, and colonial Hispanic America. Emphasis is on the art, history, and literature of these countries, including music, social customs, regional costumes, and description and travel. In this printed catalog there is at least an author card for every book in the collection printed since 1700.

New York. Public Library. *Dictionary catalog of the history of the Americas collection.* Boston: G. K. Hall, 1961. 28v.; 554,000 cards.

While the catalog of the New York Public Library's American History Room covers both North and South America, it provides a large, well-developed research collection which reflects the development of the New World from earliest times to the present. It includes entries for more than 100,000 volumes in the collection itself plus thousands of books located elsewhere in the library. The analytic entries are particularly important. For more than fifty years the library has been developing a unique reference aid through indexing important articles found in scholarly journals. The collection is particularly strong in American Indian material, in pamphlets relating to political history, and in works—old and new—which deal with discovery, exploration, and settlement.

Newberry Library. *Dictionary catalog of the Edward E. Ayer collection of Americana and American Indians.* Boston: G. K. Hall, 1961. 16v.; 169,000 cards.

Located in Chicago, this significant collection of some 90,000 volumes covers the following fields: the Indian of the Americas, North and South, from prehistory and archaeology to modern studies in ethnology and anthropology; the contact of the white man with native tribes, including 18th- and 19th-century books of travel and description which mention Indians; voyages and travels during the period of exploration and early settlement; and cartography, especially from the 15th through the 18th century.

Pan American Union. Columbus Memorial Library. *Index to Latin American periodical literature.* 1929–1960. 1st Suppl., 1961–1965. Boston: G. K. Hall, 1962, 1968. 10v.; 300,000 cards.

These volumes serve as a catalog of periodicals indexed by the Columbus Memorial Library. The periodicals are generally of Latin American origin, but may be from other parts of the world if they have articles containing information about Latin America or were done by Latin American authors. Some 800 periodicals are indexed. Subject matter is widely varied, with preference given to articles of cultural, economic, educational, historical, legal, political, and social content.

Pan American Union. Columbus Memorial Library. *Index to Latin American periodicals.* Boston: G. K. Hall, 1961 and 1962.

Although not the listing of a separate library, this general index to published information in the fields of the humanities and the social sciences is very representative of the Pan American Union's collections. Arrangement is in dictionary form by author, title, and subject entries. Subject headings appear in Spanish, with an accompanying list of corresponding English terms.

U.S. Library of Congress. Law Library. *Index to Latin*

American legislation, 1950 through 1960. Boston: G. K. Hall, 1961. 2v.; 31,000 cards.

This work covers the principal enactments in the form of laws, decrees, regulations, and administrative rulings of twenty Latin American republics. The index is arranged by country, and the entries are filed alphabetically by subject for each jurisdiction. Within each subject the entries are generally arranged chronologically.

University of Texas. Austin. Library. *Catalog of the Latin American collection.* Boston: G. K. Hall, 1970. 31v.; 560,000 cards.

This catalog represents one of the most important Latin American collections in this country. The library has more than 160,000 volumes dating from the 15th century to the present and contains information on virtually any subject relating to Latin America. In addition to the printed materials it includes non-book items, as well as an extensive collection of manuscripts, some dating back to the 16th century. The catalog is arranged as a dictionary catalog of authors, titles, and subjects for books, pamphlets, periodicals, newspapers, and microfilm.

ABBREVIATION GUIDE

AUFS	American Universities Field Staff, Inc.
L.A.	Latin America
LACAP	Latin American Cooperative Acquisitions Program
OAS	Organization of American States
PAU	Pan American Union
SALALM	Seminar on the Acquisition of Latin American Library Materials
UN	United Nations
Interlibrary loan	Indicates that this library or information center will allow its library materials to be circulated to another library for use by the distant library's patron. Also, indicates that the lending library is willing to abide by the rules and regulations of the interlibrary loan agreement code
*	Indicates country for which library is responsible under the Farmington Plan
†	Indicates photocopy services are available

LATIN AMERICAN
LIBRARY COLLECTIONS

All data on library materials are Latin Americana

UNITED STATES

1 *American Antiquarian Society. Library*
FOUNDED: 1812
ADDRESS: 185 Salisbury St.
Worcester, Mass. 01609
TELEPHONE: (617) 755-3710
LIBRARIAN: M. A. McCorison
SUBJECT STRENGTHS: historical, political, and economic conditions
10,000 + volumes on various aspects of Latin America; known
as H. R. Wagner Collection. Mainly monographic
Newspaper, early 19th century
INTERLIBRARY LOAN: no. Library open to public, but restricted to
reference use.†

2 *American Institute for Foreign Trade. Library
(Barton Kyle Memorial)*
FOUNDED: 1947
ADDRESS: P.O. Box 191
Phoenix, Ariz. 85001
TELEPHONE: (602) 938-0000, ext. 55
LIBRARIAN: Lora Jeanne Wheeler
ASST. LIBRARIAN: Ruth P. Overland
LIBRARY STAFF: 2 professionals
4 others
SUBJECT STRENGTHS: present-day economic, social, and political
conditions
5,000 + volumes
19 current periodicals
7,000 pamphlets
119 maps
7,500 documents
6 current newspapers
INTERLIBRARY LOAN: yes. Library restricted to reference use only.†

---

†Symbol indicates photocopy services are available.

27

3 *American Museum of Natural History. Library*
FOUNDED: 1903
ADDRESS: Central Park West at 79th St.
New York, N.Y. 10024
TELEPHONE: (212) TR 3-1300, ext. 333
LIBRARIAN: George H. Goodwin, Jr.
LIBRARY STAFF: 3 professionals
2 others
SUBJECT STRENGTHS: anthropology, archaeology, ethnology, and geography (expeditions and travels)
30,000 volumes
100 current periodicals
10,000 pamphlets
INTERLIBRARY LOAN: no. Library open to public, but restricted to reference use.†

4 *Arizona. State University. Library*
FOUNDED: 1891
ADDRESS: Tempe, Ariz. 85182
TELEPHONE: (602) 961-3415
LIBRARIAN: H. William Axford
SUBJECT STRENGTHS: economics, history, political science, and sociology
15,000 + volumes
120 + serials
10,000 + items on microfilm
10 newspapers
Library is developing a collection on South America
INTERLIBRARY LOAN: yes. Library open to public, but circulation restricted to students, staff, and faculty.†

5 *Arizona. University. Library*
FOUNDED: 1891
ADDRESS: Tucson, Ariz. 85721
TELEPHONE: (602) 884-2102
LIBRARIAN: Robert K. Johnson
BIBLIOGRAPHER FOR LATIN AMERICAN COLLECTIONS: Dr. Arnulfo D. Trejo

LIBRARY STAFF: 2 professionals
　　　　　　　2 others
SPECIAL COLLECTIONS: Mexican writers and music; Panama (3,000 volumes)
SUBJECT STRENGTHS: *Colombia, Mexico, and *Panama. Good history and anthropology sections
　　33,000 + volumes
　　200 + serials
　　2,000 pamphlets
　　1,400 maps
　　1,100 microforms
　　12 newspapers
　　Approximately 6 linear feet of manuscripts
Library allows interlibrary loan except for manuscripts, and is open to public but with restricted circulation.†

6　*Boston College. Libraries. Bapst Library*

FOUNDED: 1863
ADDRESS: Chestnut Hill, Mass. 02167
TELEPHONE: (617) DE 2-3200
LIBRARIAN: (Father) Brendan Connolly, S.J.
LIBRARY STAFF (part-time): 3 professionals
　　　　　　　　　　　　　4 others
SUBJECT STRENGTHS: Argentina (Levene Collection), Jamaica (Williams Collection), and ethnological collection. Argentine material is mainly social sciences, including history. Jamaican material is more general in coverage
　　9,000 volumes
　　60 current periodicals
　　Scattering of maps, photographs, and microforms
Materials circulate on interlibrary loan
Library open to public, but circulation is restricted.†

7　*Brown University. Library*

FOUNDED: 1767
ADDRESS: Providence, R.I. 02912

*Asterisk indicates country for which library is responsible under the Farmington Plan.

TELEPHONE: (401) 863-2162
LIBRARIAN: David A. Jonah
SPECIAL COLLECTION: George Earl Church Collection on South
America
SUBJECT STRENGTHS: general aspects of South America, with emphasis
on history, politics, and social conditions
15,000 + volumes
60 current periodicals
800 pamphlets
2 current newspapers
INTERLIBRARY LOAN: yes. Library open to public, but restricted to
reference use.†

8   *California. State Library. Sutro Library*
FOUNDED: 1917
ADDRESS: 2130 Fulton St.
San Francisco, Calif. 94117
TELEPHONE: (415) KL 7-0374
LIBRARIAN: Richard H. Dillon
LIBRARY STAFF: 3 professionals
SPECIAL COLLECTION: Mexican pamphlets, newspapers, and manu-
scripts (ca. 30,000 pieces) with emphasis on period of independence
SUBJECT STRENGTHS: strong on materials about Mexico, with good
collections on Brazil and South America in general. Mainly com-
merce, geography, and history-oriented collections
30,000–40,000 volumes
No current material
INTERLIBRARY LOAN: yes. Library open to public, 9:00 A.M.–6:00 P.M.
daily except Saturdays, Sundays, and holidays.†

9   *California. University. Bancroft Library*
FOUNDED: 1905
ADDRESS: University of California
Berkeley, Calif. 94720
TELEPHONE: (415) 855-6000, ext. 3781, 3782
DIRECTOR: James Skipper, Acting University Librarian
ASSIST. DIRECTOR: Robert H. Becker
LIBRARY STAFF: 7 professionals
2 others

SUBJECT STRENGTHS: areas north of the Panama Canal, particularly Mexico, the West Indies, and Venezuela. Considerable emphasis upon historical, political, and social aspects of Latin America and Mexico

    55,000 volumes
    386 periodicals
    118 documents
    4,164 reels of microfilm

Printed catalogs of books and of maps available
Library collection is noncirculating and open to reference use on a restricted basis.†

10   *California. University. Main Library*

FOUNDED: 1868
ADDRESS: Berkeley, Calif. 94720
TELEPHONE: (415) 855-6000
LIBRARIAN: James Skipper
SUBJECT STRENGTHS: historical and present-day economic, geographic, social, and political conditions. Very comprehensive coverage in the social sciences, with particular emphasis upon Brazil, *Chile, Andean region, and Mexico. Very strong anthropology collections

    100,000 + volumes
    600 + periodicals
    5,000 pamphlets
    5,000 + microforms
    10,000 + documents
    800 + maps
    15 newspapers

INTERLIBRARY LOAN: yes. Library open to public for reference use with circulation restricted to students, staff, faculty, and researchers.†

11   *California. University. Research Library*

FOUNDED: 1919
ADDRESS: Los Angeles, Calif. 90024
TELEPHONE: (213) 478-9711
LIBRARIAN: Robert Vosper
BIBLIOGRAPHER: Ludwig Lauerhass
SUBJECT STRENGTHS: South American republics, Brazil, and the Carib-

bean. Considerable strength in economics, geography, history, political science, and social conditions. Developing collections in social and cultural anthropology, especially music. Excellent map collections

  30,000 + volumes
  300 + periodicals
  2,700 pamphlets
  2,000 microforms
  15 newspapers
  3,000 + maps

Printed book catalog available

INTERLIBRARY LOAN: yes, including maps. Library open to public for reference use, with circulation restricted to students, staff, faculty, and researchers.†

12   *Catholic University of America. Oliveira Lima Library*
FOUNDED: 1916
ADDRESS: Washington, D.C. 20017
TELEPHONE: (202) 529-6000, ext. 711, 712
LIBRARIAN: Dr. Manoel S. Cardozo
LIBRARY STAFF: 1 professional
                2 others
SUBJECT STRENGTHS: Luso-Brazilian studies: history, civilization, sociology, economy, literature, and art of Portugal and Brazil. South American republics, especially Argentina. Brasiliana collection contains fine 19th-century travel books and periodicals; a collection of annual reports of the Ministry of Foreign Affairs, complete; and annals of the Senate and the Chamber of Deputies of the Imperial period

  50,000 + volumes
  30 current periodicals
  5,000 pamphlets
  400 maps, paintings, photographs, and other iconographic
      material
  60 newspaper scrapbooks

Printed book catalog available

INTERLIBRARY LOAN: no. Library open to public for reference use only. Any student of the field may use books on the premises.

Access to documents and manuscripts is restricted to qualified scholars.†

13   *Chase Manhattan Bank, North America. Library*

FOUNDED: 1919
ADDRESS: 1 Chase Manhattan Plaza
      New York, N.Y. 10015
TELEPHONE: (212) 552-4113, 4114, or 4115
LIBRARIAN: Mrs. Annchen T. Swanson
SPECIAL COLLECTIONS: business statistics and Central Bank Reports
SUBJECT STRENGTHS: economic conditions, statistics, and Central Bank reports for all countries in Latin America
    4,100 + volumes
    10 current periodicals
    7,000 + documents, pamphlets, bulletins, monthly letters, releases, and services
INTERLIBRARY LOAN: yes. Library closed to public.

14   *Chicago. University. Library*

FOUNDED: 1891
ADDRESS: 116 E. 59th St.
      Chicago, Ill. 60637
TELEPHONE: (312) MI 3-0800
LIBRARIAN: Herman H. Fussler, Director of Libraries
SUBJECT STRENGTHS: business and economics materials on most countries in Latin America. Strong collections on history, politics, and social conditions, with developing collections on urban problems
    20,000 volumes
    200 + serials
    1,800 + pamphlets
    3,700 + microforms
    10 newspapers
    Large collection of documents, manuscripts, and miscellaneous reports
INTERLIBRARY LOAN: yes. Library open to public for reference use, with circulation restricted to students, staff, faculty, and research scholars.†

15 *Clark University. Library*
FOUNDED: 1889
ADDRESS: 1 Downing St.
          Worcester, Mass. 01610
TELEPHONE: (617) 791-6241, ext. 221
LIBRARIAN: Tilton M. Barron
REFERENCE LIBRARIAN, RESPONSIBLE FOR LIBRARY SERVICE ON LATIN
  AMERICA: Marian Henderson
SUBJECT STRENGTHS: geography, economics, and history; maps
    5,000 + volumes
    20 current serials
    Small collection of documents, manuscripts, and miscellaneous
      reports
INTERLIBRARY LOAN: yes. Library open to public but circulation is
  restricted.†

16 *Columbia University. Libraries*
FOUNDED: 1761
ADDRESS: 114th St.
          New York, N.Y. 10027
TELEPHONE: (212) UN 5-4000
LIBRARIAN: Richard H. Logsdon, Director of Libraries
LIBRARY STAFF (part-time): 2 professionals
                          3 others
SPECIAL COLLECTION: inter-American relations, agreements, and
  diplomacy
SUBJECT STRENGTHS: Brazil, South American republics, Caribbean
  area. Strong economics, geography, history, and political affairs
  sections
    35,000 + volumes
    300 + serials
    1,900 + pamphlets
    5,000 + microforms
    12 newspapers
    Extensive collection of documents, manuscripts, and maps
INTERLIBRARY LOAN: yes. Library available for reference use, but
  circulation is restricted to students, staff, faculty, and qualified
  research scholars.

17 *Connecticut. University. Wilbur L. Cross Library*

FOUNDED: 1881
ADDRESS: Storrs, Conn. 06268
TELEPHONE: (203) 429-9321
LIBRARIAN: John P. McDonald
LIBRARY STAFF (part-time): 1 professional
            1 other
SUBJECT STRENGTHS: South America, Chilean history and literature
   (José Toribio Medina materials), economics, history, and social
   institutions
   7,000 + volumes
   30 + serials
   Small collection of documents, manuscripts, and miscellaneous
      reports
INTERLIBRARY LOAN: yes. Library open to public, but circulation is
   restricted to students, staff, and faculty.†

18 *Cornell University. Library*

FOUNDED: 1865
ADDRESS: Ithaca, N.Y. 14850
TELEPHONE: (607) AR 5-3689
LIBRARIAN: David Kaser
LATIN AMERICAN SPECIALIST: Glenn Reid
LIBRARY STAFF (part-time): 2 professionals
            2 others
SPECIAL COLLECTION: Brazil (Frank E. Hull Collection)
SUBJECT STRENGTHS: Brazil, Colombia, Caribbean area, *Peru. Strong
   sections in economics, anthropology, geography, history, politics,
   and social behavior
   42,000 + volumes
   150 + serials
   1,000 + pamphlets
   2,000 + microforms
   Large collection of documents, manuscripts, maps, and reports
INTERLIBRARY LOAN: yes. Library use is restricted.†

19   *Council on Foreign Relations. Foreign Relations Library*
FOUNDED: 1930
ADDRESS: 58 East 68th St.
          New York, N.Y. 10021
TELEPHONE (212) LE 5-3300
LIBRARIAN: Donald Wasson, Director
SUBJECT STRENGTHS: diplomacy, inter-American relations, and
   politics
       1,500 + volumes
       30 + serials
       Small collection of documents, pamphlets, and miscellaneous
          reports
Limited interlibrary loan granted. Library use by permission only.
Limited copying service available.

20   *Duke University. Library*
FOUNDED: 1838
ADDRESS: Durham, N.C. 27706
TELEPHONE (919) 684-2034
LIBRARIAN: Benjamin E. Powell
LIBRARY STAFF: 5 professionals
               4 others
SPECIAL COLLECTIONS: Francisco Pérez de Velasco Collection of Peru-
   viana (7,000 + volumes), Ecuadorian collection (2,000 + vol-
   umes), Brazilian collection (3,000 + volumes)
SUBJECT STRENGTHS: teaching collections for all countries of Latin
   America with in-depth research collections for *Bolivia, Brazil,
   Colombia, *Ecuador, and Peru. Strong collections in the humani-
   ties and social sciences for the above five countries
       30,000 + volumes
       250 + serials
       2,000 + microforms
       7 newspapers
       Extensive collection of documents, pamphlets, manuscripts, and
          maps
INTERLIBRARY LOAN: yes. Library open to all students and visiting
   scholars.†

21 *Fletcher School of Law and Diplomacy.*
    Edwin Ginn Library
Affiliated with Tufts University
FOUNDED: 1933
ADDRESS: Medford, Mass. 02155
TELEPHONE: (617) 776-2100
LIBRARIAN: Dorothy Fox
LIBRARY STAFF: 2 professionals
              2 others
SPECIAL COLLECTIONS: Pan American Union publications and United
  Nations Economic Committee for Latin America materials
SUBJECT STRENGTHS: Pan Americanism; U.S.–Latin American rela-
  tions; general collection on Latin America with emphasis on the
  political and economic development, social progress, and institu-
  tional reforms in Argentina, Brazil, Chile, Colombia, Mexico,
  and Venezuela
  2,500 + volumes
  23 current serial titles
  2,600 + documents
  4 current newspapers
  Miscellaneous wall maps and manuscripts
INTERLIBRARY LOAN: yes. Library open to visitors for reference use.

22 *Florida. University. Library*
FOUNDED: 1853
ADDRESS: Gainesville, Fla. 32601
TELEPHONE: (904) 376-3261, ext. 2321
LIBRARIAN: Gustave A. Harrer
ASST. DIRECTOR: John G. Veenstra
RESPONSIBLE FOR THE LATIN AMERICAN COLLECTIONS: Dr. Irene Zim-
  merman
LIBRARY STAFF: 3 professionals
              4 others
SPECIAL COLLECTIONS: Brazilian law, Caribbean area and Cuba, Latin
  American documents
SUBJECT STRENGTHS: Brazilian law, agriculture (Cuba, Caribbean
  area), documents from Latin American republics, *Bahama Is-

37

lands, *Barbados, *British Guiana, *British Honduras, *Cuba, *Dominican Republic, *French Guiana, *Guadeloupe, *Haiti, *Jamaica, *Leeward Islands, *Martinique, *Netherlands Antilles, *Surinam, *Trinidad and Tobago, *West Indies Federation, *Windward Islands

    100,000 + volumes

    1,000 current periodicals

    5,560 documents (titles)

    40 current newspapers

    Miscellaneous maps, microforms, and photographs

INTERLIBRARY LOAN: yes. Library open to public, but circulation is restricted.†

23   *Harvard University. Libraries. (Widener Memorial Library)*

FOUNDED: 1638

ADDRESS: Cambridge, Mass. 02138

TELEPHONE (617) 868-7600

LIBRARIAN: Douglas W. Bryant, University Librarian

LIBRARY STAFF (part-time): 3 professionals

                       5 others

SPECIAL COLLECTIONS: anthropology and ethnology, diplomatic relations, fine arts and letters

SUBJECT STRENGTHS: anthropology, economics, ethnology, geography, history, politics, and social conditions of most Latin American countries. Strong sections on Argentina, Brazil, Colombia, Mexico, Peru, and South America in general

    130,000 + volumes

    1,000 periodicals

    6,000 + pamphlets

    12 newspapers

    Extensive collection of documents, maps, and manuscripts

Printed book catalog of Latin America and Latin American periodicals available

INTERLIBRARY LOAN: yes. Library use is restricted.†

24   *Harvard University. Peabody Museum. Library*

FOUNDED: 1849

ADDRESS: 11 Divinity Ave.
        Cambridge, Mass. 02138
TELEPHONE: (617) 868-7600, ext. 2253
LIBRARIAN: Margaret Currier
SUBJECT STRENGTHS: archaeology and linguistics of Central America; anthropology, physical anthropology, prehistoric archaeology, and ethnology for most areas of Latin America. Strong on artifacts of Peru
    2,600 + volumes
    20 current periodicals
INTERLIBRARY LOAN: yes. Library use is restricted.†

25 *Hispanic Society of America. Library*
FOUNDED: 1908
ADDRESS: Broadway and 156th St.
        (613 West 155th St.—mailing address)
        New York, N.Y. 10032
TELEPHONE: (212) WA 6-3602
LIBRARIAN: Jean R. Longland, Curator of the Library
SUBJECT STRENGTHS: art, history, literature, and general culture of the Hispanic American countries; purchases presently being made only in the colonial field
    6,000 + volumes (documents classified as books)
    Very few current periodicals because of colonial interest
Printed book catalog available
No interlibrary loan. Library open to public, but use is restricted, especially for manuscript and early printed book materials. Restricted photocopy services.

26 *Hoover Institution on War, Revolution, and Peace. Library*
FOUNDED: 1919
ADDRESS: Stanford, Calif. 94305
TELEPHONE: (415) 321-2300
LIBRARIAN: Kenneth Glazier, Asst. Director
LATIN AMERICAN SPECIALIST: Joseph Bingaman, Asst. Librarian
SPECIAL COLLECTIONS: Mexican revolutionary posters, Cuban propaganda materials

SUBJECT STRENGTHS: Cuba, Mexico, Colombia, Central American area, and Caribbean. Diplomacy, politics, revolutionary tactics, and propaganda

    3,000 + volumes

    40 + periodicals

    Miscellaneous documents, maps, photographs, and ephemera

INTERLIBRARY LOAN: limited. Library open to visitors with permission only.†

27   *Houston. University. M. D. Anderson Memorial Library*

FOUNDED: 1934

ADDRESS: 3801 Cullen Blvd.

        Houston, Tex. 77004

TELEPHONE: (713) CA 5-4451, ext. 641, 642, or 643

LIBRARIAN: Dr. Edward G. Holley, Director of Libraries

LIBRARIAN IN CHARGE OF LATIN AMERICAN LIBRARY DEVELOPMENT: Selda Osborne

LIBRARY STAFF: 4 professionals

SUBJECT STRENGTHS: humanities and social sciences are being developed for a Latin American studies program

    10,000 + volumes

    50 current periodicals

    OAS documents

    3 newspapers

INTERLIBRARY LOAN: yes. Library open to public, with restricted circulation.†

28   *Illinois. University. Library*

FOUNDED: 1867

ADDRESS: Urbana, Ill. 61803

TELEPHONE: (217) 333-0791

LIBRARIAN: Robert B. Downs

CONSULTANT IN LATIN AMERICAN BIBLIOGRAPHY: Carl W. Deal

LIBRARY STAFF: 5 professionals

           7 others

SUBJECT STRENGTHS: humanities and social sciences, anthropology, geography, geology, history, literature, and natural history. Argentina, *Brazil, Chile, Ecuador, Mexico, and Peru, with emphasis on their history and literature

  100,000 + volumes

  2,000 current periodicals

  7 newspapers

  Extensive collection of documents, government publications, and reports

INTERLIBRARY LOAN: yes. Library open to public, but with restrictions.†

29 *Indiana. University. Library*

FOUNDED: 1824

ADDRESS: Bloomington, Ind. 47403

TELEPHONE: (812) 337-3403

LIBRARIAN: Robert A. Miller

SPECIAL COLLECTIONS: Latin America (Mendel Collection), rare books

SUBJECT STRENGTHS: anthropology, economics, geography, history, literature, and social conditions. Good literature collections and extensive works on history and politics. Argentina, Brazil, Mexico, Peru, and the Andean areas are strongly represented. Outstanding original source material on Argentina, Colombia, Ecuador, Mexico, Peru, and Venezuela, particularly historical material on the independence movement

  80,000 + volumes

  300 + current periodicals

  11 current newspapers

  Strong collection of microforms, documents, and reports

INTERLIBRARY LOAN: yes. Library open to public, but circulation is restricted. Lilly Rare Books Library is limited to use by accredited scholars and students.†

30 *Indiana University of Pennsylvania. Rhodes R. Stabley Library*

FOUNDED: 1875

ADDRESS: Indiana, Pa. 15701

TELEPHONE: (412) 463-9111, ext. 265

LIBRARIAN: William E. Lafranchi

LIBRARIAN IN CHARGE OF LATIN AMERICAN COLLECTIONS: Malcolm H. Stilson

LIBRARY STAFF: 2 professionals
3 others

SUBJECT STRENGTHS: humanities and social sciences. The library is developing a general collection for most of Latin America

4,000 + volumes
56 current periodicals
1,000 + pamphlets
1,200 + unbound serials
150 + documents
150 + maps
515 + photographs
1,000 + microforms
3 current newspapers

INTERLIBRARY LOAN: yes. Library open to public, but circulation is restricted to college faculty, staff, and students.†

31   *Johns Hopkins University. Library*

FOUNDED: 1876

ADDRESS: Charles and 34th Sts.
Baltimore, Md. 21218

TELEPHONE: (301) HO 7-3300

LIBRARIAN: John H. Berthel

SUBJECT STRENGTHS: economics, history, and politics, with good collections in diplomacy and economic cooperation between the Latin American republics. Argentina, Chile, Colombia, and the Central American republics are well represented

50,000 + volumes
200 + current periodicals
1,000 + microforms
7 current newspapers
Good collection of documents, maps, pamphlets, and economic reports

INTERLIBRARY LOAN: yes. Library open to public for reference use, but circulation is restricted to faculty, students, and staff.†

32   *Kansas. University. Library*

FOUNDED: 1866

ADDRESS: Lawrence, Kans. 66044

TELEPHONE: (913) UN 4-3601

LIBRARIAN: David W. Heron

LATIN AMERICAN CATALOGER: Dr. Gilberto Fort

LIBRARY STAFF: 1 professional
                       1 other

SPECIAL COLLECTIONS: Brazilian and Portuguese language and literature; general economics and history; and Costa Rican materials
in all subject areas

SUBJECT STRENGTHS: economics, history, language, and literature;
Argentina, Colombia, *Costa Rica, Mexico, and Peru. Library is
developing a Brazilian collection

   25,000 + volumes

   200 + current periodicals

   5 current newspapers

INTERLIBRARY LOAN: yes. Library open to public, but with restricted
circulation.†

33   *Kent State University. Library*

FOUNDED: 1913

ADDRESS: Kent, Ohio 44240

TELEPHONE: (216) 672-2962

LIBRARIAN: Hyman Kritzer, Director of Libraries

LIBRARY STAFF: 3 professionals

SPECIAL COLLECTION: General Records of the U.S. Dept. of State
(RG59); Microfilm Materials on Cuba (from the National Archives)

SUBJECT STRENGTHS: history of Mexico; U.S. relations with Latin
American countries

   10,000 + volumes

   100 + current periodicals

   1,000 + documents

   2 newspapers

INTERLIBRARY LOAN: yes. Library open to the public.†

34   *Library of International Relations*
FOUNDED: 1932
ADDRESS: 660 North Wabash Ave.
          Chicago, Ill. 60611
TELEPHONE: (312) SU 7-7928
LIBRARIAN: Eloise Requa, Director
SUBJECT STRENGTHS: politics and government, population, natural
  resources, economic conditions, foreign policy, and international
  and regional organizations. Countries well represented are Ar-
  gentina, Brazil, and Mexico; materials being developed on Cen-
  tral American republics
    27,000 + volumes
    150 current periodicals
    20,000 + bound periodicals
    26,000 pamphlets
    35,000 + documents
    250 + maps
    4 Vertical File cabinets of indexed ephemera
INTERLIBRARY LOAN: no. Library use restricted.

35   *Los Angeles. Public Library*
FOUNDED: 1878
ADDRESS: 630 West Fifth St.
          Los Angeles, Calif. 90017
TELEPHONE: (213) 626-7461
LIBRARIAN: Harold L. Hamill
SUBJECT STRENGTHS: major historical works on all Latin American
  countries; bibliographies and significant works on Amerindian
  archaeology and ethnology, including codices. Strong collections
  on Mexico and Lower California
    20,000 + volumes
    200 + current periodicals
    2 current newspapers
INTERLIBRARY LOAN: yes. Library open to public.†

36   *Miami. University. Richter Library*
FOUNDED: 1926

44

ADDRESS: Coral Gables, Fla. 33124
    (P.O. Box 8214—mailing address)
    Coral Gables, Fla. 33124
TELEPHONE: (305) MO 1-2511
LIBRARIAN: Archie L. McNeal
LIBRARY STAFF (part-time): 2 professionals
               3 others
SUBJECT STRENGTHS: economic conditions, diplomacy, and history of Latin America in general. Strong collections on Colombia, Jamaica, and the Caribbean region. Library is at present developing a collection on Cuba, stressing mainly the social sciences and literature
    16,000 + volumes
    150 + current periodicals
    4 newspapers
    Large collection of documents, manuscripts, maps, and reports
INTERLIBRARY LOAN: yes. Library open to public for reference use, with circulation restricted to students, faculty, and staff.†

37   *Michigan. University. University Library*

FOUNDED: 1838
ADDRESS: Ann Arbor, Mich. 48104
TELEPHONE: (313) 764-9366
LIBRARIAN: Frederick H. Wagman
SUBJECT STRENGTHS: economics and history, with good collections in anthropology, diplomacy, geography, politics, and social conditions. Extensive language and literature collections, with some linguistic materials. Brazil and Mexico are well represented, with good coverage for most South American republics
    67,000 + volumes
    1,200 + current periodicals
    3,000 + pamphlets
    500 + maps
    7 newspapers
    1,500 + reels of microfilm, including OAS documents
INTERLIBRARY LOAN: yes, except for certain manuscripts and rare materials. Library open to public, but circulation is restricted to faculty, students, staff, and visiting scholars.†

38 *Michigan. University. William L. Clements Library*

FOUNDED: 1923

ADDRESS: Ann Arbor, Mich. 48104

TELEPHONE: (313) 764-2347

LIBRARIAN: Howard H. Peckham

SPECIAL COLLECTIONS: manuscript collections are described in *A Guide to the Manuscript Collections in the Clements Library*, 1953, compiled by William S. Ewing. Manuscripts are mainly historical and relate chiefly to Mexico

SUBJECT STRENGTHS: history, diplomacy, social conditions, and literature. Good manuscript holdings on Mexico

    1,500 + volumes

    Large number of maps

    Unquantified number of manuscripts, approximately 1,000

    Miscellaneous documents, reports, and other ephemeral items

No interlibrary loan. Library use is restricted to scholars; collections are restricted to reference use.†

39 *Michigan State University. Library, and International Division*

FOUNDED: 1855 (Internat. Div. founded 1963)

ADDRESS: East Lansing, Mich. 48823

TELEPHONE: (517) 355-2366 and 355-2341

LIBRARIAN: Richard E. Chapin

HEAD, INTERNATIONAL DIVISION: Eugene de Benko

BIBLIOGRAPHER FOR LATIN AMERICAN STUDIES: Tamara Brunnschweiler

LIBRARY STAFF: 2.75 professionals

              1.50 others

SPECIAL COLLECTIONS: 2,300 + pamphlets in the International Division dealing with economic, social, and political conditions in Latin America and economic, social, and political assistance and training offered by governmental and nongovernmental agencies from the United States

SUBJECT STRENGTHS: history and social sciences are stressed with Argentina, Brazil, Colombia, and Mexico securing emphasis. Strong collection of documents, pamphlets, reports, and other ephemeral items dealing with the process of economic development and education

24,000 + volumes
1,000 + current periodicals and bulletins
2,300 + pamphlets
1,500 maps
1,000 + microforms
9 newspapers
INTERLIBRARY LOAN: yes. Library open to public.†

40   *Minnesota. University. Libraries*
FOUNDED: 1851
ADDRESS: Minneapolis, Minn. 55455
TELEPHONE: (612) 373-3082
LIBRARIAN: Edward B. Stanford, Director of Libraries
LIBRARY STAFF (part-time): 2 professionals
                          2 others
SUBJECT STRENGTHS: economics, government, and politics, particularly inter-American relations. Argentina, Brazil, Chile, Colombia, Ecuador, Mexico, and Peru are well represented. Fairly good
   literature sections
   20,000 + volumes
   300 + current periodicals
   600 + pamphlets
   1,000 + microforms and documents
   5 newspapers
INTERLIBRARY LOAN: yes. Library open to public, but circulation is
   restricted to faculty, students, and staff.†

41   *Missionary Research Library*
SUPPORTED BY: Division of Overseas Ministries, National Conference
   of Catholic Charities–USA, and Union Theological Seminary
FOUNDED: 1941
ADDRESS: 3041 Broadway
         New York, N.Y. 10027
TELEPHONE: (212) MO 2-7100, ext. 417
DIRECTOR: Robert F. Beach
LIBRARIAN: Mrs. Margaret Wang
SUBJECT STRENGTHS: religion, Christian missions and churches, and
   social and political aspects of missionary work in Latin America

70,000 + volumes (about 30% deal with L.A.)
800 + current periodicals (about 40% deal with L.A.)
30,000 + pamphlets (about 30% deal with L.A.)
INTERLIBRARY LOAN: yes. Library open to public, but circulation is
   restricted.

42   *New Mexico. University. Zimmerman Library*
FOUNDED: 1892
ADDRESS: Albuquerque, N.M. 87106
TELEPHONE: (505) 277-4241
LIBRARIAN: David Otis Kelley
BIBLIOGRAPHER FOR LATIN AMERICAN COLLECTIONS: Helen McIntyre
LIBRARY STAFF: 3 professionals
SPECIAL COLLECTIONS: Coronado materials; especially strong in Portuguese language and literature
SUBJECT STRENGTHS: history, geography, economics, government, anthropology, and archaeology in Argentina, Brazil, Colombia, and
   Mexico. Very good collection on Latin America in general
   27,000 + volumes
   1,200 + current periodicals and bulletins
   1,000 + pamphlets
   20,000 + documents
   2,000 + maps
   1,000 + reels of microfilm
   5 current newspapers
INTERLIBRARY LOAN: yes. Library open to public, but circulation is
   restricted to faculty, staff, and students.†

43   *New York. City College. M. R. Cohen Library*
FOUNDED: 1850
ADDRESS: 135th St. and Convent Ave.
         New York, N.Y. 10031
TELEPHONE: (212) AD 4-2000, ext. 272
LIBRARIAN: Dr. Bernard Kreissman
SUBJECT STRENGTHS: history, government and politics, language and
   literature
   4,000 + volumes
   55 + current periodicals

INTERLIBRARY LOAN: yes. Library open to public, but restricted to reference use.†

44   *New York. State University at Stony Brook.*
   Frank J. Melville Memorial Library

FOUNDED: 1957

ADDRESS: Stony Brook, Long Island, N.Y. 11790

LIBRARIAN: Ruben Weltsch

SUBJECT STRENGTHS: colonial and current history, social sciences, and literature. Strong holdings of Argentine, Brazilian, and Mexican materials, with general interest in all areas of Latin America

   25,000 + volumes

   100 + current periodicals

   Small collection of documents, maps, and ephemera

   Parral microfilm and Medina microfilm

INTERLIBRARY LOAN: yes. Open to public, but circulation restricted to faculty, students, and staff.

45   *New York Public Library. Astor, Lenox and Tilden*
   Foundation. Research Libraries

FOUNDED: 1895

ADDRESS: Fifth Ave. and 42d St.

   New York, N.Y. 10011

TELEPHONE: (212) OX 5-4200

DIRECTOR OF LIBRARY: Edward G. Freehafer

CHIEF, RESEARCH LIBRARIES: James W. Henderson

SUBJECT STRENGTHS: all social sciences, humanities, and fine arts except law, medicine, theology, pedagogy, and biological sciences. Good comprehensive collections on all Latin American republics

   Total number of volumes not quantified, but in excess of 100,000

   Total number of current periodicals not quantified, but in excess of 100

   1,500 + documents

   6 current newspapers

Printed book catalog of the History of the Americas collection available

No interlibrary loan. Library open to public for reference use only.†

46 *New York University. Library*

FOUNDED: 1835

ADDRESS: Washington Square
New York, N.Y. 10003

TELEPHONE: (212) SP 7-2000

LIBRARIAN: Charles F. Gosnell

SPECIAL COLLECTION: Latin American writers and poets, especially Brazilian literature

SUBJECT STRENGTHS: commerce, economics, history, humanities, international relations, and literature. Particularly strong in materials from Argentina, Brázil, Colombia, and Mexico
20,000 + volumes
150 + current periodicals
1,600 documents, maps, and ephemeral items
5 current newspapers

INTERLIBRARY LOAN: yes. Library open to public, but circulation is restricted to faculty, students, and staff.†

47 *North Carolina. University. Louis R. Wilson Library*

FOUNDED: 1795

ADDRESS: Chapel Hill, N.C. 27514

TELEPHONE: (919) 933-1301

LIBRARIAN: Dr. Jerrold Orne

LIBRARIAN FOR LATIN AMERICAN STUDIES: Dr. Berta Becerra

SUBJECT STRENGTHS: history, literature, political and social sciences. Areas of concentration include Argentina, Chile, Paraguay, Uruguay, and Venezuela (main area of interest)
40,000 + volumes
450 current periodicals
18,000 + pamphlets
530 + documents
PAU microforms
4 current newspapers

INTERLIBRARY LOAN: yes. Library open to public, but circulation is restricted to faculty, students, and staff.†

48 *Northwestern University. Libraries*

FOUNDED: 1856

ADDRESS: Evanston, Ill. 60201

TELEPHONE: (312) 492-5217

LIBRARIAN: Thomas R. Buckman

SPECIAL COLLECTION: Bolivian historical manuscripts (ca. 40,000 pieces)

SUBJECT STRENGTHS: anthropology, ethnology, geography, history, language and literature, and political science. Argentina, Bolivia, Chile, Mexico, and Peru are well represented with especially good holdings on Brazil

    16,000 + volumes

    135 + current periodicals

    2,000 + maps

    4,700 + microforms

    4 newspapers

INTERLIBRARY LOAN: yes. Library open to public, but circulation restricted to faculty, students, and staff.†

49 *Notre Dame University. Libraries*

FOUNDED: 1873

ADDRESS: Notre Dame, Ind. 46556

TELEPHONE: (219) 284-7317

LIBRARIAN: James W. Simonson

SPECIAL COLLECTION: Zahm South American Library (1,600 + volumes)

SUBJECT STRENGTHS: history, geography, government, and social institutions. Good area collections on Argentina, Chile, Mexico, and particularly Brazil

    8,900 + volumes

    100 + current periodicals

    2,000 + maps and photographs

    500 + microforms

INTERLIBRARY LOAN: yes, but not on Zahm Library materials. Library open to public with restricted use of certain items.†

50 *Ohio State University. Libraries*

FOUNDED: 1873

ADDRESS: 1858 Neil Ave.

       Columbus, Ohio 43210

TELEPHONE: (614) 293-6152

LIBRARIAN: Lewis C. Branscomb

LIBRARY STAFF: 2 professionals

SUBJECT STRENGTHS: South America, Central America, Mexico, Caribbean, and small island groupings in the Caribbean

> Total number of volumes not quantified, but in excess of 10,000
>
> Total number of current periodicals not quantified, but in excess of 50
>
> 200 + maps
>
> 2 newspapers
>
> Miscellaneous and scattered collection of documents and microforms

INTERLIBRARY LOAN: yes. Library open to public with circulation restricted to faculty, students, and staff.†

51 *Oklahoma. University. Libraries*

FOUNDED: 1892

ADDRESS: Norman, Okla. 73069

TELEPHONE: (405) JE 6-0900, ext. 2031

LIBRARIAN: Arthur McAnally

GEOGRAPHY-GOVERNMENT-HISTORY AND AREA LIBRARIAN: Opal Carr

LIBRARY STAFF: 1 professional

SUBJECT STRENGTHS: geography, government, history, and politics of Latin America in general. Developing collection on Brazil

> Total number of volumes not quantified, but in excess of 12,000
>
> 120 + current periodicals

INTERLIBRARY LOAN: yes. Library open to public, but circulation restricted to faculty, students, and staff.†

52 *Oregon. University. Libraries*

FOUNDED: 1881

ADDRESS: Eugene, Ore. 97403

TELEPHONE: (503) 342-1411

LIBRARIAN: Carl W. Hintz

SUBJECT STRENGTHS: business, economics, geography, and history of Latin America in general. Good collections on Argentina, Colombia, and Mexico. Business and economic interest in Central American republics

> 13,700 + volumes

200 + periodicals

INTERLIBRARY LOAN: yes. Library open to public, but circulation restricted to faculty, students, and staff.†

53   *Pan American Union. Columbus Memorial Library*

FOUNDED: 1890

ADDRESS: 17th and Constitution Aves.

Washington, D.C. 20006

TELEPHONE: (202) DU 1-8254, 8259, or 8408

LIBRARIAN: Arthur E. Gropp

ASSOC. LIBRARIAN: Marietta Daniels Shepard

ACQUISITIONS LIBRARIAN: Peter J. de la Garza

LIBRARY STAFF: 23 professionals

12 others

Entire collection is Latin Americana, with subject strengths in: art, bibliography, biography, economics, education, history, law, library science, literature, music, philology, philosophy, political science, social sciences, statistics, and travel

210,000 + volumes

3,000 + current periodicals

3,000 + maps

27,000 + photographs

Microforms on UN and OAS documents

1 or 2 newspapers from each country in Latin America

Printed catalogs of periodical literature and of periodicals available

INTERLIBRARY LOAN: yes. Library open to public with reading-room use of materials only. OAS employees (i.e., Pan American Union) are given priority over outside users.†

54   *Panama Canal Company—Canal Zone Government. Canal Zone Library*

FOUNDED: 1914

ADDRESS: Box M

Balboa Heights, Canal Zone

TELEPHONE: Balboa 4326

LIBRARIAN: Emily J. Price

LIBRARY STAFF: 4 professionals

2 others

SPECIAL COLLECTION: Panama collection, concerned with the history of the Isthmus and of interoceanic canals. Subject catalog of this collection was published in 1964 by G. K. Hall and Co.

SUBJECT STRENGTHS: Latin American history, politics, travel, and social conditions. Argentina and Mexico along with Panama are best-represented areas

    30,000 + volumes

    50 + current periodicals

    250 + maps on Panama

    5,000 + photographs on Panama

    Panama Star & Herald on microfilm, 1849–1914

    2 newspapers (from Panama)

INTERLIBRARY LOAN: no. Library open to public, but circulation restricted to U.S. government employees or residents of the Canal Zone.†

55   *Pennsylvania. State University. Pattee Library*

FOUNDED: 1857

ADDRESS: University Park, Pa. 16802

TELEPHONE: (814) 865-2112

LIBRARIAN: W. Carl Jackson

LATIN AMERICAN SPECIALIST: Edgar E. Cordoba

SUBJECT STRENGTHS: Hispanic and Luzo-Brazilian literature and history. Collection is currently being developed in the social sciences

    8,000 + volumes

    100 + current bulletins and periodicals

    200 + maps

    PAU and OAS documents depositories

    1 newspaper

INTERLIBRARY LOAN: yes. Library open to public, but circulation restricted to faculty, students, and staff.†

56   *Pennsylvania. University. Libraries*

FOUNDED: 1750

ADDRESS: 3420 Walnut St.

        Philadelphia, Pa. 19104

TELEPHONE: (215) 594-7092

LIBRARIAN: Kenneth M. Setton

SUBJECT STRENGTHS: economics, history, international law, and political behavior of Latin American republics. Good collection of language and literature. Areas of concentration include Argentina, Colombia, Mexico, and particularly Brazil

　11,700 + volumes
　120 + current periodicals
　5,000 + microforms
　1,000 + documents and maps
　5 newspapers

INTERLIBRARY LOAN: yes. Library open to public, but circulation restricted to faculty, students, and staff.†

57　*Pennsylvania. University. Museum. Library*

FOUNDED: 1887
ADDRESS: 33d and Spruce Sts.
　　　　Philadelphia, Pa. 19104
TELEPHONE: (215) EV 6-7400
LIBRARIAN: Cynthia Griffin
SUBJECT STRENGTHS: anthropology and archaeology of Middle and South America, with some materials on ethnology

　1,500 + volumes
　27 + current periodicals
　Miscellaneous collection of documents, reports, bulletins, and
　　manuscripts
　Good collection of artifacts and photographs

INTERLIBRARY LOAN: yes, only for books. Library open to public, but circulation is restricted.†

58　*Pittsburgh. University. Libraries*

FOUNDED: 1787
ADDRESS: 4200 Fifth Ave.
　　　　Pittsburgh, Pa. 15213
TELEPHONE: (412) 621-2500, ext. 242
LIBRARIAN: C. Walter Stone, Director
LATIN AMERICAN BIBLIOGRAPHER: Eduardo Lozano
LIBRARY STAFF: 1 professional
　　　　　　　2 others

SPECIAL COLLECTIONS: Biblioteca Andreana: 24,000 volumes on Latin
   American poetry, drama, and Mexican revolution; 3,000 volumes
   on Bolivia
SUBJECT STRENGTHS: humanities and social sciences for Latin America
   in general, with good representative collections from all Latin
   American republics. Particularly strong in history, economics, and
   political science. Strong collections on Bolivia, Brazil, and Mexico
      75,000 + volumes
      200 + current periodicals
      1,000 + pamphlets
INTERLIBRARY LOAN: yes. Library open to public, but circulation is
   restricted to qualified borrowers as stipulated in the library's lending code.†

59 *Population Reference Bureau. Library*
FOUNDED: 1929
ADDRESS: 1755 Massachusetts Ave., N.W.
            Washington, D.C. 20036
TELEPHONE: (202) 232-2288
LIBRARIAN: Arlene M. Joy
LIBRARY STAFF: 2 professionals
SUBJECT STRENGTHS: all materials dealing with population and de-
   mography of Latin America. Economics, geography, and sociology
   are best represented. Library is in the process of reclassifying
   Latin American material
      1,500 + volumes
      20 current periodicals
      Good collection of miscellaneous documents, reports, bulletins,
      and other ephemera dealing with population and demog-
      raphy
INTERLIBRARY LOAN: yes. Library open to public, but circulation is
   restricted.

60 *Princeton. University. Library*
FOUNDED: 1746
ADDRESS: Princeton, N.J. 08540
TELEPHONE: (609) 452-3181
LIBRARIAN: William S. Dix

BIBLIOGRAPHER FOR LATIN AMERICA AND THE IBERIAN PENINSULA: Barbara H. Stein

SPECIAL COLLECTIONS: Gates Collection: 270 pre-Columbian codices in manuscript format. Kane Collection: includes 133 early editions of pre-1800 titles. Marquand Library of Art: index of ancient American architecture (13,000 photographs), 2,000 slides of pre-Columbian art objects. Scheide Library: includes a collection of pre-1600 Mexican and Peruvian imprints

SUBJECT STRENGTHS: colonial architecture, economics, economic history, history, literature, political science, and pre-Columbian art. Comprehensive collections on Argentina, Brazil, Chile, Cuba, Mexico, and Venezuela, with general collections on the West Indies and Latin America in general

    36,500 + volumes

    650 + current periodicals

    900 + pamphlets

    3,000 + maps

    100 + microforms

    6 current newspapers

INTERLIBRARY LOAN: yes. Library open to public, but circulation is restricted to faculty, students, staff, and those who have obtained borrowing privileges.†

61   *Rutgers—The State University. Library*

FOUNDED: 1766

ADDRESS: College Ave.

       New Brunswick, N.J. 08903

TELEPHONE: (201) CH 7-1766

LIBRARIAN: Roy Kidman

LATIN AMERICAN BIBLIOGRAPHER: Francis Johns

LIBRARY STAFF: 2 professionals

            4 others

SPECIAL COLLECTIONS: Argentine labor material. Confédération Générale du Travail 1932–1955

SUBJECT STRENGTHS: Argentina, Brazil, and Mexico, with Argentine holdings quite strong. 20th-century history, government, and social conditions for Argentina, Brazil, and Mexico, with general coverage for other Latin American republics

20,000 + volumes
300 + current periodicals
1,000 + pamphlets
100 + documents
50 microforms
3 current newspapers

INTERLIBRARY LOAN: yes. Library open to public, but circulation restricted to faculty, students, and staff.†

62   *Southwest Museum, Inc. Library*

FOUNDED: 1907
ADDRESS: Highland Park, Los Angeles, Calif. 90042
TELEPHONE: (213) 221-2163
LIBRARIAN: Mrs. Charlotte T. Tufts
LIBRARY STAFF: 1 professional
             2 others
SPECIAL COLLECTIONS: comprehensive collection on pre-American California; serial publications on Mexican archaeology; collection of facsimiles of Mexican codices and their commentaries
SUBJECT STRENGTHS: anthropology and history, with greatest strengths on Mexico and Central America and emphasis on Mexico
    Total number of volumes unquantified, but in excess of 1,000
    30 + current periodicals
    3,000 + pamphlets
    300 + maps
    6,000 + photographs
    5 current newspapers
INTERLIBRARY LOAN: restricted. Library open to public but restricted to reference use. No photocopying services available.

63   *Stanford University. Libraries*

FOUNDED: 1891
ADDRESS: Stanford, Calif. 94305
TELEPHONE: (415) 321-2300
LIBRARIAN: David Weber
CURATOR FOR LATIN AMERICAN PUBLICATIONS : James Breedlove

LIBRARY STAFF: 4 professionals
            3 others
SUBJECT STRENGTHS: Brazil and Mexico have special strengths, with all Latin America well represented. Strong subject collections in economics, education, geology, government publications, history, and political behavior. Humanities, the social and behavioral sciences, agriculture, and music are also being developed
    50,000 + volumes
    300 + current periodicals
    32 current newspapers
    Strong collection of maps, documents, and microforms in excess of 5,000 + items
INTERLIBRARY LOAN: yes. Library use restricted to faculty, students, and staff. Others may use the collections upon payment of fee.†

64 *Syracuse University. Libraries*
FOUNDED: 1870
ADDRESS: Syracuse, N.Y. 13210
TELEPHONE: (315) GR 6-5571
LIBRARIAN: Warren N. Boes, Director
SUBJECT STRENGTHS: education, geography, history, journalism, political science, and public administration. Good general coverage for most of Latin America (*Paraguay, *Uruguay) with strongest collections on *Argentina, Brazil, and Mexico
    15,000 + volumes
    80 + current periodicals
    500 + maps
    1,000 + documents and reports
    300 + microforms
    4 newspapers
INTERLIBRARY LOAN: yes. Library open to public, but circulation restricted to students, staff, and faculty.†

65 *Texas. University. Mirabeau B. Lamar Library*
FOUNDED: 1883
ADDRESS: Austin, Tex. 78712
TELEPHONE: (512) GR 1-3811
LIBRARIAN: Fred Folmer

LIBRARIAN OF THE LATIN AMERICAN COLLECTION: Nettie Lee Benson
LIBRARY STAFF: 10 professionals
                15 others
SPECIAL COLLECTIONS: Hugo F. Kuehne Collection of books and
    plates on colonial Spanish and Mexican architecture (Architecture
    Library); Edward Laroque Tinker Library—relates to the Horse-
    men of the Americas collection; Texas collection; Genaro Garcia
    Collection; Music Library—microfilm of rare cathedral music from
    Mexico City; newspaper collection—includes many newspapers,
    primarily Mexican; plus 15 other separate special collections
SUBJECT STRENGTHS: inclusive coverage, on a broad basis, for all
    countries in Latin America, including *Costa Rica and all Carib-
    bean islands. Especially rich in materials relating to Guatemala,
    *Mexico, Paraguay, and the adjacent Río de la Plata area; strong
    coverage for Brazil, Chile, and northern sections of South Amer-
    ica. Subjects represented best are bibliography, history, literature,
    and the social sciences
    200,000 + volumes
    1,000 + current periodicals and bulletins
    400 + photographs
    4,200 reels of microfilm
    575,000 pages of manuscripts
    2,000 broadsides
    6,000 slides in the art collection
    1,700 maps plus 3,000 in Dept. of Geography map collection
Printed book catalog of Latin American collection available
INTERLIBRARY LOAN: yes. Library open to public, but circulation re-
    stricted to faculty, students, staff, and scholars.†

66 *Texas. University, at El Paso. Library*

FOUNDED: 1913
ADDRESS: P.O. Box 180
         El Paso, Tex. 79999
TELEPHONE: (915) 542-5672
LIBRARIAN: Baxter Polk
LIBRARY STAFF: 2 professionals
SPECIAL COLLECTIONS: John H. McNeely Collection of Latin Ameri-
    cana; Juárez (Chihuahua) archives; Archivo de Hidalgo de Parral;

Archivo General de la Nación de México; Archivo Histórico Diplomático Mexicano

SUBJECT STRENGTHS: very good collections on Mexico, with developing collections on Central America and, to a lesser degree, South American republics. The social sciences, history, and diplomacy are strongest subject areas

    7,000 + volumes

    25 + current periodicals

    150 + pamphlets

    100 + documents

    1 newspaper

INTERLIBRARY LOAN: yes. Library open to public, but circulation is restricted to faculty, students, and staff.†

67   *Tulane University. Middle American Research Institute. Latin American Library*

FOUNDED: 1924

ADDRESS: New Orleans, La. 70118

TELEPHONE: (504) 865-7711, ext. 7628

LIBRARIAN: John Gribbin, Director

HEAD, LATIN AMERICAN LIBRARY: Marjorie LeDoux

LIBRARY STAFF: 3 professionals
               3 others

SPECIAL COLLECTION: Gates Collection (Central American anthropology, ethnology, and history)

SUBJECT STRENGTHS: Central America is strongest geographical area of concentration (*El Salvador, *Guatemala, *Honduras, *Nicaragua) with developing collections in South America, especially those areas contingent to Central America. Social sciences, with particular emphasis on anthropology, ethnology, and history, are best represented

Total of 85,000 + items are available (no library statistical breakdown available)

INTERLIBRARY LOAN: yes. Library open to public, with restricted circulation.

68   *United Fruit Company. Central Research Laboratories Library*

FOUNDED: 1958

ADDRESS: Upland Road
     Norwood, Mass. 02062
TELEPHONE: (617) DA 6-6650
LIBRARIAN: Anne D. Andrews
SPECIAL COLLECTIONS: bananas, banana plants, and their diseases
SUBJECT STRENGTHS: good collections on the geography and history
    of Central America, with developing collection on travel and
    travels in this region
        1,200 + volumes
        25 + current periodicals
        1,180 + documents, reports, and bulletins
No interlibrary loan. Open to public by permission, with reference
use of materials available only.

69   *United Nations. Dag Hammarskjöld Library*

FOUNDED: 1946
ADDRESS: United Nations Plaza
    New York, N.Y. 10017
TELEPHONE: (212) PL 4-1234
LIBRARIAN: L. I. Vladimirov
SUBJECT STRENGTHS: Latin America in general, with particular inter-
    est in inter-American relations, politics, statistics, and economic
    conditions of each Latin American republic
        Total number of volumes not quantified, but in excess of 15,000
        2,000 + microforms and documents
        100 + current periodicals
        Strong map collection
        Good selection of newspapers
INTERLIBRARY LOAN: restricted. Library open to public, but available
    for reference use only.†

70   *United States. Department of State. Library*

FOUNDED: 1789
ADDRESS: Washington, D.C. 20520
TELEPHONE: (202) DU 3-2181
LIBRARIAN: Fred W. Shipman
SUBJECT STRENGTHS: materials from all Latin American republics are
    acquired. Library stresses all phases of political, economic, social,

and cultural conditions and particularly the history of each country. Collection is also strong in the fields of international law and international relations, and a special effort is made to collect official documents

60,000 + volumes

Figures on number of current periodical titles, microforms, and reports are not available. The collection of documents is very strong, as is the newspaper collection

INTERLIBRARY LOAN: yes. Library open to serious students of a graduate level or above who find themselves in need of materials not available from public sources. No duplicating facilities available.

Three major U.S. government libraries in the Washington, D.C., area should be mentioned. Because of the vast holdings of all three libraries, quantitative information is not available. However, each library possesses noteworthy collections and subject holdings on one or more subjects and countries in Latin America that should not be overlooked by the serious student and scholar:

U.S. Library of Congress. Hispanic Section
  Washington, D.C. 20540
  Telephone: (202) 426-5397

U.S. National Archives and Record Service. Library
  Washington, D.C. 20408
  Telephone: (202) 963-6745

U.S. Smithsonian Institution. Libraries
  Washington, D.C. 20560
  Telephone: (202) 381-5382

The student and scholar should direct their questions concerning Latin American library materials at these libraries to the Latin American specialist at each library.

Printed book catalog (Library of Congress) of Latin American legislation (1950–60) available.

71   *University of Southern California. Library*
FOUNDED: 1880
ADDRESS: University Park
           Los Angeles, Calif. 90007
TELEPHONE: (213) 746-2540
LIBRARIAN: Lewis F. Stieg
SUBJECT STRENGTHS: education, history, political science, and sociology. Very strong collections on international relations, public administration, and development administration. All Latin American countries, especially Mexico and Brazil, are well represented. Collections are being developed in the humanities and other social science areas
      30,000 + volumes
      110 + current periodicals
      2,000 documents
      2 newspapers
INTERLIBRARY LOAN: yes. Library open to public, but circulation is restricted to faculty, staff, students, and qualified scholars.†

72   *Utah. University. Libraries*
FOUNDED: 1850
ADDRESS: Salt Lake City, Utah 84112
TELEPHONE: (801) 322-6741
LIBRARIAN: Ralph D. Thomson, Director
LIBRARY STAFF: 4 professionals
SPECIAL COLLECTIONS: OAS documents; Readex Hispanic and Portuguese bibliographies; and Archivo de Hidalgo de Parral microfilm materials
SUBJECT STRENGTHS: Mexico, Central America, and Brazil are well represented and under development, with emphasis on history and literature. Developing collection on anthropology
      5,000 + volumes
      150 + current periodicals
      250 + pamphlets
      1,200 + documents
      500 + maps
      1,000 + microforms
      6 current newspapers
INTERLIBRARY LOAN: yes. Library open to public, but circulation re-

stricted to faculty, students, staff, and holders of library card which may be purchased for $10 per year.†

73   *Vanderbilt University, Peabody College, and Scarritt College. Joint University Libraries*

FOUNDED: 1936

ADDRESS: 21st Ave., South
        Nashville, Tenn. 37203

TELEPHONE: (615) 254-1429, ext. 7351, 7352

LIBRARIAN: Frank P. Grisham

CATALOGER IN CHARGE OF LIBRARY SERVICE ON LATIN AMERICA: Stella Smock

SUBJECT STRENGTHS: Brazil, with emphasis on the humanities and social sciences, especially history and social conditions. Colombia, also with emphasis on the humanities and social sciences. Chile, with particular strength in the social sciences, especially political and social conditions

    10,000 + volumes
    100 + current periodicals
    500 + pamphlets
    200 + documents, maps, and photographs
    200 + reels of microfilm
    3 current newspapers

INTERLIBRARY LOAN: yes. Library open to public, but circulation is restricted to faculty, students, and staff.†

73a   *Virginia. University. Alderman Library*

FOUNDED: 1819

ADDRESS: Charlottesville, Va. 22903

TELEPHONE: (703) 295-2166

LIBRARIAN: Ray W. Frantz

SUBJECT STRENGTH: *Venezuela

NOTE: The above information was gleaned from secondary sources. It is included here, rather than in the Addenda, because the library is responsible for Venezuela under the Farmington Plan.

74   *Washington. State University. Library*

FOUNDED: 1890

ADDRESS: Pullman, Wash. 99163

TELEPHONE: (509) ED 5-4539

LIBRARIAN: G. Donald Smith

CHIEF, SOCIAL SCIENCE LIBRARY (LATIN AMERICAN SPECIALIST): George J. Rausch, Jr.

LIBRARY STAFF: 2 professionals
             2 others

SPECIAL COLLECTION: Regla Papers (manuscript collection of a prominent Mexican family covering several centuries)

SUBJECT STRENGTHS: general coverage for all Latin America with relatively strong holdings on the history of most of the republics. Greatest strength is in Mexican history and institutions
    16,000 + volumes
    100 + current periodicals
    1,000 pamphlets
    1,000 + documents
    1,000 + microcards
    2 newspapers

INTERLIBRARY LOAN: yes. Library open to public, but circulation is restricted to faculty, students, and staff.†

75   *Washington. University. Libraries*

FOUNDED: 1861

ADDRESS: Seattle, Wash. 98105

TELEPHONE: (206) 543-1760

LIBRARIAN: Marion A. Milczewski, Director

SUBJECT STRENGTHS: economics, geography, political science, population, and statistics. Good, general coverage for South American republics, with Argentina, Brazil, and Chile best represented
    Total number of volumes not quantified, but in excess of 15,000
    100 + current periodicals
    800 + documents
    300 + microforms

INTERLIBRARY LOAN: yes. Library open to public, but circulation restricted to faculty, students, and staff.†

76   *Washington University. Libraries*

FOUNDED: 1853

ADDRESS: Skinker and Lindell Blvds.
         Saint Louis, Mo. 63130

TELEPHONE: (314) VO 3-0100

LIBRARIAN: Andrew J. Eaton, Director

ASST. DIRECTOR OF LIBRARIES (LATIN AMERICAN SPECIALIST): William Kurth

SUBJECT STRENGTHS: anthropology, archaeology, history, political and social conditions. Brazil and Mexico are receiving current development

    17,000 + volumes

    120 + current periodicals

INTERLIBRARY LOAN: yes. Library open to public for reference use only. Circulation restricted to faculty, students, and staff.†

77 *Wisconsin. University. Memorial Library*

FOUNDED: 1850

ADDRESS: Madison, Wis. 53706

TELEPHONE: (608) 262-3521

LIBRARIAN: Louis Kaplan

SUBJECT STRENGTHS: agricultural economics, economic conditions, commerce, history, and international relations for most of Latin America. Mainly general coverage of South American republics, with Argentina, Brazil, Colombia, and Mexico best represented. Presently developing collections in literature and social conditions

    20,000 volumes

    130 + current periodicals

    1,000 + documents, reports, and bulletins

    Good collection of maps and microform materials

INTERLIBRARY LOAN: yes. Library open to public, but circulation restricted to faculty, students, and staff.†

78 *Yale University. Sterling Memorial Library*

FOUNDED: 1701

ADDRESS: 120 High St.

    New Haven, Conn. 06520

TELEPHONE: (203) 787-3131, ext. 353 (Librarian);

    ext. 779 (Latin American collection)

LIBRARIAN: Rutherford D. Rogers

LIBRARIAN, LATIN AMERICAN COLLECTION: Mrs. Nelly Ermili

LIBRARY STAFF: 1 professional

            4 others

SPECIAL COLLECTIONS: Hiram Bingham Collection (history and geography, 2,000 vols.; Peru, 2,000 vols.; Yale–National Geographic Peruvian Expeditions); Henry Raup Wagner Collection (South American economics and metallurgy, 6,430 vols.; Mexico: 10,000 vols., 2,600 broadsides and folios, 155 newspapers, and 134 periodicals); Carlos Alfredo Tornquist Collection (500 + vols. on major Argentine authors); Lindley and Charles Eberstadt Collection; Ernesto Stelling Collection; Collection from the Second Mexican Empire; Argentine politics and government

SUBJECT STRENGTHS: in-depth and strong coverage of all Central and South American countries, particularly Argentina, *Costa Rica, Mexico, and Peru, with increasing strength in Brazil. Strongest fields represented are economics, history, politics and government, and description and travel

    50,000 + volumes
    670 + current periodicals
    5,200 + pamphlets
    67 documents (titles)
    1,955 + maps
    8 current newspapers

INTERLIBRARY LOAN: yes, for materials in the stacks. Library open to public, but circulation restricted to faculty, students, staff, and paying users.†

PUERTO RICO

79 *Caribbean Economic Development Corporation.*
Regional Library

FOUNDED: 1946
ADDRESS: 452 Avenida Ponce de León
        Hato Rey, P.R. 00919
        (Box 1058, Hato Rey, P.R. 00919—mailing address)
TELEPHONE: 767-0250
LIBRARIAN: Paulita Maldonado
LIBRARY STAFF: 2 professionals
           3 others
SPECIAL COLLECTIONS: UN, European Economic Community, OAS, and all Caribbean countries government documents

SUBJECT STRENGTHS: agriculture, economics, education, business, trade, and tourism for Puerto Rico and the Caribbean area

75,000 + volumes

200 + current periodicals

1,800 + microforms

5 newspapers

35 Vertical File containers of ephemeral materials

INTERLIBRARY LOAN: yes. Circulation is restricted.†

80 *Inter American University of Puerto Rico. Libraries*

FOUNDED: 1923

ADDRESS: San German, P.R. 00753

TELEPHONE: 892-1095, ext. 216

LIBRARIAN: Laurence Miller

SUBJECT STRENGTHS: Puerto Rico and the Caribbean are areas of greatest interest. Economics, history, government, and social conditions are major fields of interest

7,000 + volumes

75 current periodicals

1,700 microforms

4 newspapers

INTERLIBRARY LOAN: yes. Library open to public, but circulation restricted to faculty, students, and staff.†

81 *Puerto Rico. State Archives. Libraries*

FOUNDED: 1955

ADDRESS: 305 San Francisco St.

San Juan, P.R. 00905

TELEPHONE: 724-2138

LIBRARIAN: Fernando Labault

SUBJECT STRENGTHS: history and political and social institutions of Puerto Rico and Caribbean area

10,000 + volumes

100 + current periodicals

1,700 + microforms

INTERLIBRARY LOAN: yes. Library open to public, with circulation of materials restricted.

82   *Puerto Rico. University. Libraries*

FOUNDED: 1903

ADDRESS: Río Piedras, P.R. 00931

TELEPHONE: 766-0000, ext. 208

LIBRARIAN: Josefina del Toro

IN CHARGE OF PUERTO RICAN COLLECTION: Dr. Emilio Colón

SPECIAL COLLECTIONS: Juan Ramón Jiménez Puerto Rican collection,
   and Caribbean studies materials

SUBJECT STRENGTHS: Puerto Rico, the Caribbean, Central America,
   and Mexico are well represented, with a growing interest in Cuba.
   Anthropology, ethnology, history, government, and social conditions, particularly for Puerto Rico and the Caribbean area, are
   well represented
   30,000 + volumes
   700 + current periodicals
   3,000 + microforms
   5 newspapers
   Good collection of maps and government publications

INTERLIBRARY LOAN: yes. Library open to public, but circulation restricted to faculty, students, and staff.†

VIRGIN ISLANDS

83   *College of the Virgin Islands. Library*

FOUNDED: 1963

ADDRESS: Box 1826
         Saint Thomas, V.I. 00802

TELEPHONE: 4-1252

LIBRARIAN: Ernest C. Wagner

SUBJECT STRENGTHS: Virgin Islands and the West Indies, with folklore, history, politics, and social conditions best represented.
   Folklore materials on the West Indies are under development
   2,000 + volumes
   32 + current periodicals
   Developing collection of documents, reports, and bulletins

INTERLIBRARY LOAN: yes. Library open to public, but circulation restricted to faculty, students, and staff.†

84   *Department of Education. Bureau of Libraries and Museums*

FOUNDED: 1920
ADDRESS: Box 390, Charlotte Amalie
        Saint Thomas, V.I. 00802
TELEPHONE: 744-0630
CHIEF LIBRARIAN: Enid M. Baa
SPECIAL COLLECTIONS: old and rare Caribbean maps; Virgin Islands
  newspapers dating back to 1770 available on microfilm
SUBJECT STRENGTHS: Caribbean history, with emphasis on the Virgin
  Islands
    1,800 + volumes
    29 + current periodicals and bulletins
No interlibrary loan. Library open to public but circulation is
  restricted.

CANADA

85   *Royal Bank of Canada. Library*

FOUNDED: 1913
ADDRESS: P.O. Box 6001
        Montreal 1, Quebec, Can.
TELEPHONE: (514) 874-2272
LIBRARIAN: Miriam H. Tees
SUBJECT STRENGTHS: economic conditions of Latin America including
  all types of statistical information, with business and commerce
  the strongest areas
    800 + volumes
    83 + periodicals
    1,500 pamphlets
INTERLIBRARY LOAN: yes. Library open to public, but circulation is
  restricted.†

86   *Toronto. University. Libraries*

FOUNDED: 1841
ADDRESS: Toronto 5, Ontario, Can.
TELEPHONE: (416) 926-2294

LIBRARIAN: Robert H. Blackburn

IN CHARGE OF BOOK SELECTION FOR LATIN AMERICA: David Esplin, Asst. Librarian

SUBJECT STRENGTHS: literature is strongest area; colonial era and the 19th century are most strongly represented. Developing collections in geography and political science. Mexico and the Caribbean areas have been favored, with Brazil well represented, especially in geographic and government publications

    19,000 + volumes

    700 + periodicals

    1,000 + pamphlets

    100 + documents

    2,000 + maps

    6 current newspapers

INTERLIBRARY LOAN: yes. Nonstudents, staff, or faculty must register with the library and have a serious reason for requesting access to the collections.†

87   *American Universities Field Staff, Inc.*

FOUNDED: 1951

ADDRESS: 366 Madison Ave.
New York, N.Y. 10017

TELEPHONE: (212) YU 6-6722

DIRECTOR: Teg C. Grondahl, Executive Director

SUPPORT: corporation, composed of 12 educational institutions, provides 34% of supporting funds; Ford Foundation grant, 36%; other income 30%

PURPOSE: to conduct a continuing study of political, economic, and social developments in Asia, Africa, Eastern Europe, and Latin America

RESEARCH FIELDS: socioeconomic change, accomplished mostly through individual research for *AUFS Reports,* supplemented by formal quantitative research and staff-written collaborative studies

PROPORTION OF RESEARCH ON LATIN AMERICA: 20%

PUBLICATIONS: AUFS Reports (two series on Latin America) and books

RESEARCH STAFF: 12 professionals
8 others

LATIN AMERICAN RESEARCH SPECIALISTS: 3.

No interlibrary loan. Use of library restricted.

88   *American University. Cultural Information Analysis Center*

FOUNDED: 1956

ADDRESS: 5010 Wisconsin Ave., N.W.
Washington, D.C. 20016

DIRECTOR: Preston S. Abbott

Part of the American University's Center for Research in Social Systems

SUPPORT: U.S. Dept. of the Army

PURPOSE: identification and bibliographic control of social science literature; reports of completed and ongoing research in the social sciences; and the preparation of responses to inquiries on the regional literature of Asia, Latin America, and the Middle East–Africa

RESEARCH FIELDS: cultural anthropology, economics, history, military sciences, political science, social anthropology, social psychology, sociology, and statistics

PROPORTION OF RESEARCH ON LATIN AMERICA: 15%

PUBLICATIONS: CRESS studies and reports

RESEARCH STAFF: 73

LATIN AMERICAN RESEARCH SPECIALISTS: 12

LIBRARIAN: Jack M. Watson, Jr., Chief, Information Systems Branch
   6,000 + books
   650 + current periodicals
   2,000 + documents, pamphlets, reports, etc.

Library is not open to public except with the permission of the Chief of the Information Systems Branch for special projects; otherwise, library restricted to research staff

INTERLIBRARY LOAN: yes.†

89 *Amerind Foundation, Inc.*

FOUNDED: 1937

ADDRESS: Dragoon, Ariz. 85609

TELEPHONE: (602) 586-3003

DIRECTOR: Charles C. Di Peso

SUPPORT: privately endowed, self-supporting foundation

PURPOSE: conducts archaeological and ethnohistorical research in the American Southwest and northern Mexico

RESEARCH FIELDS: anthropology, archaeology, ethnology, and history

PROPORTION OF RESEARCH ON LATIN AMERICA: 60% on Mexico (northern)

PUBLICATIONS: Monographic series, no.1–9

RESEARCH STAFF: 3 professionals
          5.5 others

LATIN AMERICAN RESEARCH SPECIALISTS: 1

LIBRARIAN: Mrs. Ruth B. Rinaldo
   8,000 + volumes
   35 + current periodicals
   1,060 + pamphlets

Library stresses archaeology and history of Mexico and Latin America. Restricted to researchers. No interlibrary loan.†

90 *Arizona. State University. Center for Latin American Studies*
FOUNDED: 1965
ADDRESS: Tempe, Ariz. 85281
TELEPHONE: (602) 966-5058
DIRECTOR: Marvin Alisky
Integral unit of the College of Liberal Arts
SUPPORT: State University provides 90% of funds; gifts, grants, subscriptions, 10%
PURPOSE: to publish *Latin American Digest* of political, economic, and social trends and news; to assist the Arizona State University Library in acquiring books and documents on Latin America; to aid M.A. and Ph.D. students doing research in Latin American demographic area.
RESEARCH FIELDS: politics, economics, and social trends
PROPORTION OF RESEARCH ON LATIN AMERICA: 100%
PUBLICATIONS: *Latin American Digest* (bimonthly)
RESEARCH STAFF: 10 professionals (part-time)
                2 others
Center maintains a reading room with 25 current newspapers and magazines.

91 *Arizona. University. Latin American Studies Program*
FOUNDED: 1953
ADDRESS: Tucson, Ariz. 85721
TELEPHONE: (602) 634-8181, ext. 321
DIRECTOR: Dr. Renato Rosaldo
CODIRECTOR: Prof. Juan B. Rael from Stanford University
SUPPORT: semiautonomous body financed from student fees
PURPOSE: to conduct a summer school at Guadalajara, Jalisco, Mexico; to offer students a chance to study, live, and become acquainted with the culture of Mexico
RESEARCH FIELDS: Mexican anthropology, culture, history, and social institutions

RESEARCH STAFF: 40 professionals (part-time)
                2 others
LATIN AMERICAN SPECIALISTS: 14
Maintains a pocket-library collection of 500 + volumes devoted almost exclusively to Mexico.

92 *Beloit College. Logan Museum of Anthropology*

FOUNDED: 1892
ADDRESS: Beloit, Wis. 53512
TELEPHONE: (608) 365-3391
DIRECTOR: Dr. Andrew Hunter Whiteford
Integral unit of Beloit College
SUPPORT: Beloit College, 60%; foundations, 20%; private sources, 20%
PURPOSE: teaching of anthropology and techniques of anthropological research; preservation and exhibition of anthropological materials; and promulgation of anthropological research
RESEARCH FIELDS: archaeological excavations in Central Mexico; social-anthropological research in Colombia, Mexico, and Central America
PROPORTION OF RESEARCH ON LATIN AMERICA: 70%
PUBLICATIONS: Logan Museum *Bulletins*
RESEARCH STAFF: 5 professionals
                4 others
LATIN AMERICAN RESEARCH SPECIALISTS: 3.

93 *Brigham Young University. BYU–New World Archaeological Foundation*

FOUNDED: 1952
ADDRESS: Provo, Utah 84601
TELEPHONE: (801) 374-1211
DIRECTOR: Gareth W. Lowe
Autonomous unit
SUPPORT: 100% financial support from Brigham Young University
PURPOSE: to conduct cultural historical research in Mesoamerica with special concentration on the beginnings of civilization in this area

RESEARCH FIELDS: archaeology, ethnology, and history for
    Mesoamerica
PUBLICATIONS: papers of the New World Archaeological Foundation
RESEARCH STAFF: 6 professionals
                8 others
LATIN AMERICAN RESEARCH SPECIALISTS: 4
Foundation maintains a small library composed of:
    400 + volumes
    15 + current periodicals
    8 professional journals
    100 + pamphlets
    Miscellaneous materials include original research notes, site
        records,'and photographic file
Library stresses anthropology of Mesoamerica. Open to any research
    scholar. No interlibrary loan.†

94   *Brookings Institution. Foreign Policy Studies Program*

FOUNDED: 1946
ADDRESS: 1775 Massachusetts Ave., N.W.
        Washington, D.C. 20036
TELEPHONE: (202) HU 3-8919
DIRECTOR: H. Field Haviland, Jr., Director of Foreign Policy Studies
Integral unit of Brookings Institution
SUPPORT: 60% supporting funds from parent institution, 40%
    support from foundation grants
PURPOSE: to conduct studies of selected problems of U.S. foreign
    policy
RESEARCH FIELDS: economic, social, and political problems of the
    emerging countries as related to U.S. policy; U.S. policy problems
    concerning the United Nations and the specialized agencies
PROPORTION OF RESEARCH ON LATIN AMERICA: 50%
PUBLICATIONS: Brookings Institution studies and special series
RESEARCH STAFF: 15 professionals
                7 others
LATIN AMERICAN RESEARCH SPECIALISTS: 6 professionals
LIBRARIAN: Virginia Whitney
The Institution maintains a special library:
    40,000 + volumes

350 + current periodicals
3 newspapers
6 journals
Library restricted to use by Brookings Institution staff.

95   *California. University. Berkeley. Center for
Latin American Studies*
FOUNDED: 1956
ADDRESS: Berkeley, Calif. 94720
TELEPHONE: (415) 845-6000, ext. 2088
CHAIRMAN: Robert W. Anderson
Integral unit of the Institute of International Studies
SUPPORT: 90% supporting funds from parent institution, 10% other
PURPOSE: to conduct research on all aspects of political and socio-
economic change in Latin America
RESEARCH FIELDS: social sciences and humanities, including studies of
comparative bureaucracies, authority in a developing area, and
urban planning
PROPORTION OF RESEARCH ON LATIN AMERICA: 100%
RESEARCH STAFF: 1 professional
                1 other.

96   *California. University. Berkeley. International
Population and Urban Research*
FOUNDED: 1956
ADDRESS: Berkeley, Calif. 94720
TELEPHONE: (415) 845-6000, ext. 3450
DIRECTOR: Kingsley Davis
Autonomous unit associated with the Institute of International
Studies on the Berkeley campus
SUPPORT: major portion of supporting funds comes from private and
government sources
PURPOSE: devoted to the scientific study of population dynamics,
urbanization, and related topics
RESEARCH FIELDS: demography in general, population studies, most
aspects of urban studies, and urban sociology
PROPORTION OF RESEARCH ON LATIN AMERICA: 90%
PUBLICATIONS: Reprint series (available on demand)

RESEARCH STAFF: 8 professionals
                7 others
LATIN AMERICAN RESEARCH SPECIALISTS: 3
LIBRARIAN: Mrs. V. Moses
    4,100 + volumes
    40 + current periodicals
    300 + pamphlets
    Small microfilm collection on Latin America
Library restricted to research staff.

97   *California. University. Los Angeles. Center for the
     Study of Comparative Folklore and Mythology*
FOUNDED: 1960
ADDRESS: Los Angeles, Calif. 90024
TELEPHONE: (213) 478-9711, ext. 2985
DIRECTOR: Wayland D. Hand
Integral unit of the University of California at Los Angeles
SUPPORT: 80% support from parent institution, 20% from research
    foundations
RESEARCH FIELDS: folk belief and superstition, folk music, folk
    legend, comparative mythology, and folklore in general
PROPORTION OF RESEARCH ON LATIN AMERICA: 15%. Center has a
    Latin American program under development
PUBLICATIONS: *Folklore Americas,* a journal sponsored by the Center
RESEARCH STAFF: 10 professionals
                10 others
LATIN AMERICAN RESEARCH SPECIALISTS: 2
LIBRARIAN: Jeanette Menaugh
    5,000 + volumes
    30 + current periodicals
    50,000 + documents
    10,000 + pamphlets
Stresses Latin American folktales, folk beliefs, and folk music
Library restricted to use by research staff.

98   *California. University. Los Angeles. Institute of
     Ethnomusicology*
FOUNDED: 1961

ADDRESS: Los Angeles, Calif. 90024
TELEPHONE: (213) 478-9711, ext. 3241 or 272-8911, ext. 2980
DIRECTOR: Mantle Hood
Integral unit of the University of California at Los Angeles
SUPPORT: 50% support funds from Department of Music, 50% from
   Ford Foundation
PURPOSE: to provide space and resources for advanced graduate and
   special students for research of non-Western musics
RESEARCH FIELDS: specific musical cultures and specific aspects of
   those cultures. Investigation of non-Western music from a scien-
   tific, analytical standpoint, using specially designed and built
   electronic equipment
PROPORTION OF RESEARCH ON LATIN AMERICA: 10%
RESEARCH STAFF: 8 full-time persons
                     additional part-time help
LATIN AMERICAN RESEARCH SPECIALISTS: 3
LIBRARIAN: Mrs. Ann Briegleb
   1,500 + books
   10 + current periodicals
   1,000 + pamphlets
   4,000 + tapes and phonograph recordings
Stresses music and musical cultures of Latin America
Library restricted to use by ethnomusicology students and faculty.

99 *California. University. Los Angeles. Latin American Center*

FOUNDED: 1959
ADDRESS: Los Angeles, Calif. 90024
TELEPHONE: (213) 478-9711, ext. 3192
DIRECTOR: Johannes Wilbert
BIBLIOGRAPHER: Martin Sable
Integral unit of the University of California at Los Angeles
SUPPORT: 75% from University funds, 25% extramural
PURPOSE: to conduct interdisciplinary training and research
   concerning Latin America
RESEARCH FIELDS: social sciences, humanities, bibliography, and
   interdisciplinary studies. Urban studies, community development,
   and regional development

PROPORTION OF RESEARCH ON LATIN AMERICA: 100%, with Mexico,
   Brazil, Chile, and Venezuela securing greatest attention
PUBLICATIONS: Monographic series
                Reference series
RESEARCH STAFF: 5 professionals
                10 others
Maintains a special reference library restricted to use by Center staff.

100   *Catholic University of America. Institute of Ibero-American Studies*

FOUNDED: 1932
ADDRESS: Washington, D.C. 20017
TELEPHONE: (202) 729-6000
DIRECTOR: Michael Kenny
Separate unit of Catholic University—affiliated with it, but with its
   own board of control
SUPPORT: 80% from parent organization, 20% other sources
PURPOSE: to conduct research and investigation on all aspects of
   Ibero-American culture and problems
RESEARCH FIELDS: current social science problems and inter-
   disciplinary research in the humanities
RESEARCH STAFF: 11
PROPORTION OF RESEARCH ON LATIN AMERICA: 79%
LATIN AMERICAN RESEARCH SPECIALISTS: 6.

101   *Chicago. University. Center for Latin American Economic Studies*

FOUNDED: 1965
ADDRESS: Department of Economics
         University of Chicago, Chicago, Ill. 60637
TELEPHONE: (312) 643-0800, ext. 3846
DIRECTOR: Arnold C. Harberger
Integral unit of the Department of Economics
SUPPORT: 100% funds provided by Ford Foundation
PURPOSE: to provide for Latin American graduate students of eco-
   nomics, and other graduate students interested in Latin American
   problems, a curriculum directly relevant to types of problems
   encountered in Latin American countries; to provide a continuing

flow of high-quality research on Latin American economic problems

RESEARCH FIELDS: economic conditions and problems, including income, employment, taxation, development planning and policy, economic aspects of international relations, and economic history

PROPORTION OF RESEARCH ON LATIN AMERICA: 100%

RESEARCH STAFF: 4 professionals
              1 other

LATIN AMERICAN RESEARCH SPECIALISTS: 4.

102 *Colorado. University. International Economic Studies Center*

FOUNDED: 1962

ADDRESS: Boulder, Colo. 80302

TELEPHONE: (303) 443-4877, ext. 7337

DIRECTOR: Wyn F. Owen

Integral unit of the University of Colorado

SUPPORT: U.S. Dept. of State, 70% supporting funds; Rockefeller Foundation, 25%; parent institution, 5%

PURPOSE: to sponsor research and investigation on instructional change on a cooperative basis directly related to international economic conditions and business relationships

RESEARCH FIELDS: international economics and business

PROPORTION OF RESEARCH ON LATIN AMERICA: 90%

RESEARCH STAFF: 4 professionals
              2 others

LATIN AMERICAN RESEARCH SPECIALISTS: 2.

103 *Columbia University. Institute of Latin American Studies*

FOUNDED: 1961

ADDRESS: 417 West 117th St.
         New York, N.Y. 10027

TELEPHONE: (212) 280-4643

DIRECTOR: Charles Wagley

ASSOC. DIRECTOR: Kempton E. Webb

Integral unit of Columbia University and one of several regional institutes within Columbia University's School of International Affairs

SUPPORT: 30% from National Defense Education Act, 70% from parent institution and Ford Foundation funds

PURPOSE: to promote a better understanding of the contemporary problems of Latin American nations and a more knowledgeable basis for inter-American relations. Trains M.A. and Ph.D. students

RESEARCH FIELDS: anthropology, geography, government, history, political science, and sociology, with additional work on socio-economics and literature; mainly social sciences

PROPORTION OF RESEARCH ON LATIN AMERICA: 100%

RESEARCH STAFF: 18 professionals
4 others

LIBRARIAN: Mrs. Hilda Labrada

Maintains a small library for use by institute staff and students. Bulk of Latin American library materials are in the main library collections.

104 *Committee for Economic Development*

FOUNDED: 1942

ADDRESS: 711 Fifth Ave.
New York, N.Y. 10022

TELEPHONE: (212) 688-2063

PRESIDENT: Alfred C. Neal

Autonomous, self-supporting organization

PURPOSE: to conduct research and formulate policy recommendations on major economic issues

RESEARCH FIELDS: balance of payments; fiscal, monetary, and debt management; international economic policy; transportation; economic and regional development; urban problems; and business education

PROPORTION OF RESEARCH ON LATIN AMERICA: 10–15%

PUBLICATIONS: occasional reports (policy studies)
supplementary reports (irregular)

RESEARCH STAFF: 40

LATIN AMERICAN RESEARCH SPECIALISTS: 4

Maintains a special library for members of CED research staff use.

105 *Council on Foreign Relations, Inc.*

FOUNDED: 1921

ADDRESS: Harold Pratt House
58 East 68th St.
New York, N.Y. 10021
TELEPHONE: (212) 535-3300
DIRECTOR: George S. Franklin, Jr., Executive Director
ASSOC. EXECUTIVE DIRECTOR FOR PROGRAM: David W. MacEachron
Autonomous, self-supporting corporation
PURPOSE: to study all aspects of U.S. foreign policy (including the nature of programs) and the difficult problems which must be met, suggesting opportunities for U.S. action; to provide a meaningful exchange of opinion between foreigners and U.S. government officials; and to increase understanding of foreign-policy issues
RESEARCH FIELDS: commerce, economics, government, politics, social conditions, and international relations and diplomacy
PROPORTION OF RESEARCH ON LATIN AMERICA: 10–20%
PUBLICATIONS: *Foreign Affairs* (quarterly)
    United States in World Affairs (annual)
    Documents in American Foreign Relations (annual)
    Political Handbook and Atlas of the World (annual)
    occasional publications
RESEARCH STAFF: 30 professionals
    50 others
LATIN AMERICAN RESEARCH SPECIALISTS: 2
Maintains a special library:
LIBRARIAN: Donald Wasson
    9,700 volumes
    15 current periodicals and newspapers
    45,000 documents (UN and OAS)
Library open to scholars upon application. Interlibrary loan.

106 *Florida. University. Center for Latin American Studies*

FOUNDED: 1963
ADDRESS: Gainesville, Fla. 32601
TELEPHONE: (904) 376-3261, ext. 2224
DIRECTOR: Lyle N. McAlister
Integral unit of the University of Florida
SUPPORT: parent institution, 90%; other funds, 10%

PURPOSE: to conduct research on political and socioeconomic problems of Latin America, including, initially, the political role of
the military
RESEARCH FIELDS: economics, government, history, politics, sociology,
and development problems, particularly in the Caribbean area
PROPORTION OF RESEARCH ON LATIN AMERICA: 100%
RESEARCH STAFF: 3 professionals
2 others
PUBLICATIONS: occasional monographs and reports.

107 *Heye Foundation. Museum of the American Indian*
FOUNDED: 1916
ADDRESS: Broadway at 155th St.
New York, N.Y. 10032
TELEPHONE: (212) AU 3-2420
DIRECTOR: Frederick J. Dockstader
Autonomous institution
SUPPORT: 100% of funds from private endowment
PURPOSE: exhibition, study, and preservation of the material cultures
of all indigenous tribes of the Americas
RESEARCH FIELDS: archaeology, ethnology, and bibliography
PROPORTION OF RESEARCH ON LATIN AMERICA: 35%
RESEARCH STAFF: 3 professionals
4 others
LATIN AMERICAN RESEARCH SPECIALISTS: 1
Maintains a special library:
LIBRARIAN: Nancy Strowbridge
35,000 + volumes
100 + current periodicals
5,000 + pamphlets
3 current newspapers
Library stresses all areas—prehistoric and modern—of Latin America.
Open to use by serious students. Interlibrary loan.

108 *Illinois. University. Center for Latin American
Studies*
FOUNDED: 1959
ADDRESS: Urbana, Ill. 61803

TELEPHONE: (217) 333-3182
DIRECTOR: John Thompson
Integral unit of the University of Illinois
SUPPORT: parent institution, 90%; U.S. Office of Education and
other sources, 10%
PURPOSE: to conduct interdisciplinary research on Latin America and
provide instructional assistance to advanced students
RESEARCH FIELDS: mainly social sciences, with some research in
history and literature
RESEARCH STAFF: 25 professionals
5 others.

109 *Indiana University. Latin-American Studies. Program*

FOUNDED: 1954
ADDRESS: Bloomington, Ind. 47405
TELEPHONE: (812) 337-5450
DIRECTOR: James R. Scobie
Integral unit of the area studies program of Indiana University
SUPPORT: Indiana University Foundation, 10%; parent institution,
60%; Ford Foundation, 30%
PURPOSE: to provide coordination of research and exchange pro-
grams with Latin American institutions and to supervise the M.A.
program and the B.A. and Ph.D. certificate programs in Latin
American Studies
RESEARCH FIELDS: national period, Mexican history; contemporary
Caribbean and Cuban relations; national period, Argentine his-
tory, literature, and linguistics; Brazilian anthropology and
archaeology; Peruvian anthropology, economic development, and
socioeconomic conditions; political party structure in Argentina
and Brazil; music, musicology, folk music, and folk art of Latin
America
RESEARCH STAFF: 28 professionals
PUBLICATIONS: Latin American Monograph series of Indiana
University Press.

110 *Institute of Public Administration*

FOUNDED: 1906

ADDRESS: 55 West 44th St.
         New York, N.Y. 10036
TELEPHONE: (212) 661-2540
DIRECTOR: Lyle C. Fitch, President
Autonomous, self-supporting organization
SUPPORT: grants from foundations; contracts with federal, state, and
   local government agencies
RESEARCH FIELDS: urbanism, municipal development and administra-
   tion; training for public administration–government service abroad
PROPORTION OF RESEARCH ON LATIN AMERICA: 70% of international
   program
RESEARCH STAFF: 43 professionals
               20 others
LATIN AMERICAN RESEARCH SPECIALISTS: 15
PUBLICATIONS: IPA occasional monographs, reports, and bulletins
Maintains a special library:
   14,200 + volumes
   74 + current periodicals
   4,500 + pamphlets (included in volume count)
Library open to public. Interlibrary loan.

111   *Inter-American Bibliographical and Library Association*

FOUNDED: 1930
ADDRESS: P.O. Box 583
         North Miami Beach, Fla. 33160
TELEPHONE: (none)
DIRECTOR: A. Curtis Wilgus, President
Affiliated with the University of Florida
SUPPORT: internal funding, 20%; publications, donations, sales, and
   endowments, 80%
PURPOSE: to compile and publish bibliographies; cooperate with
   libraries and inter-American organizations; and give assistance in
   finding materials on Latin America and related topics
RESEARCH FIELDS: social sciences and humanities, library science, and
   bibliography
RESEARCH STAFF: 3
PUBLICATIONS: *Doors to Latin America* (quarterly).

112   *Louisiana. State University. Graduate Program in Latin American Studies*

FOUNDED: 1960
ADDRESS: Baton Rouge, La. 70803
TELEPHONE: (504) DI 8-6511, ext. 5101
DIRECTOR: M. Lee Taylor, Chairman
Integral unit of Louisiana State University
SUPPORT: parent institution, 85%; U.S. government, 10%; other, 5%
PURPOSE: to conduct research and coordinate instruction and training on Latin America
RESEARCH FIELDS: anthropology, archaeology, economics, foreign languages, geography, government, history, and sociology
RESEARCH STAFF: 18 professionals
            2 others.

113   *Massachusetts Institute of Technology. Center for International Studies*

FOUNDED: 1951
ADDRESS: 50 Memorial Drive
            Cambridge, Mass. 02137
TELEPHONE: (617) 864-6900, ext. 3121
DIRECTOR: Max F. Millikan
Integral unit of Massachusetts Institute of Technology
SUPPORT: parent institution, 5%; foundations, 50%; contracts from various government departments, 45%
PURPOSE: to conduct research in the social sciences on international affairs
RESEARCH FIELDS: economics, international communication, international Communist movement, political development, and U.S. military and foreign policy
PROPORTION OF RESEARCH ON LATIN AMERICA: 10%
PUBLICATIONS: occasional papers
RESEARCH STAFF: 41 professionals
            44 others (part-time)
LATIN AMERICAN RESEARCH SPECIALISTS: 9
Maintains a special library:

LIBRARIAN: Patricia Carey
3,000 + volumes
220 + current periodicals
200 + pamphlets
25 current newspapers
7 Latin American newspapers and periodicals.

114 *Miami University. Research Institute for Cuba and the Caribbean*

FOUNDED: 1966
ADDRESS: P.O. Box 8123
Coral Gables, Fla. 33124
TELEPHONE: (305) 661-2511
DIRECTOR: Mose L. Harvey
Integral unit of the Miami University Center for Advanced International Studies
SUPPORT: parent institution, 90%; other sources, 10%
PURPOSE: to conduct investigations and make available research studies on socioeconomic problems in Cuba and the Caribbean area
RESEARCH FIELDS: economics, geography, migration of population, political conditions and problems, and social conditions and problems in Cuba and the Caribbean area
RESEARCH STAFF: 8 professionals, 5 supporting professionals
2 others.

115 *Minnesota. University. Center for International Relations and Area Studies*

FOUNDED: 1948
ADDRESS: Minneapolis, Minn. 55455
TELEPHONE: (612) 373-2691
DIRECTOR: Burton M. Sapin
Integral unit of the University of Minnesota
SUPPORT: parent institution, 100%
PURPOSE: to coordinate program in international relations and area studies; to maintain and provide information on various areas of the world, especially Asia and Latin America; and to provide training and employment opportunities for students

RESEARCH FIELDS: social sciences, mainly, with economics, public administration, international relations, and interdisciplinary program in area studies

PROPORTION OF RESEARCH ON LATIN AMERICA: 10%

RESEARCH STAFF: 4 professionals
             1 other

LATIN AMERICÁN RESEARCH SPECIALIST: 1

Maintains a special library:
  1,500 + volumes
  200 current periodicals
  6 newspapers
  6,000 + documents
  5,000 + pamphlets

SPECIAL COLLECTION: Asher Christiansen Collection of Latin American books and documents emphasizing Argentina

Library open to public. Interlibrary loan.

116   *Museum of New Mexico. Research Laboratory*

FOUNDED: 1930; associated with Museum of New Mexico in 1947

ADDRESS: P.O. Box 2087
             Santa Fe, N.M. 87501

TELEPHONE: (505) 827-2732

DIRECTOR: Delmar M. Kolb

CURATOR IN CHARGE OF THE RESEARCH DIVISION: Alfred E. Dittert, Jr.

Integral unit of the Museum of New Mexico, a state-supported institution

SUPPORT: parent institution, 80%; grants, contracts, gifts, and other sources, 20%

PURPOSE: to conduct research programs related to exhibits in all units of the museum; to cooperate with federal, state, and private agencies in conducting archaeological investigations; to obtain funds for problem-oriented research; and to provide contractual services for other institutions in such studies as pollen analysis, cultural geology, and the like

RESEARCH FIELDS: archaeology, environmental research, social anthropology, and the preservation of cultural artifacts. Cooperation with the museum's International Folk Art unit, resulting in research on folk art and culture

PROPORTION OF RESEARCH ON LATIN AMERICA: varies; usually in excess
   of 70%
PUBLICATIONS: occasional monographs, studies, and series published
   by the Museum of New Mexico Press
RESEARCH STAFF: 17 professionals
                  5 others + part-time help
LATIN AMERICAN RESEARCH SPECIALISTS: 4 + 2 members of the
   International Folk Art unit
LIBRARIAN: Mrs. Bryan
Maintains a library composed of five major collections, Morley
   Library being devoted entirely to Latin America. Total library
   holdings:
     70,000 + volumes
     100 + periodicals
     30 + newspapers
Library open to public.

117   *New York. City University. Center for Latin*
      American Studies
FOUNDED: 1963
ADDRESS: City University of New York
           111 Convent Ave.
           New York, N.Y. 10031
TELEPHONE: (212) 234-2000
DIRECTOR: José María Chaves
Integral unit of City University of New York
SUPPORT: parent institution, 80%; foundations and other funds, 20%
PURPOSE: to conduct research on Latin America of an interdisci-
   plinary nature, with emphasis upon the Caribbean area, and to
   disseminate the results of such investigations
RESEARCH FIELDS: anthropology, cultural conditions, literature, and
   socioeconomic conditions. Primary interest is Puerto Rico and the
   Caribbean area
PUBLICATIONS: occasional studies and reports, with most papers and
   articles made available in established journals
RESEARCH STAFF: 20 professionals (part-time)
                  4 others
Maintains a small library collection restricted to staff use.

118   *New York. State University. Center for Inter-
      American Studies*
FOUNDED: 1962
ADDRESS: 1223 Western Ave.
         Albany, N.Y. 12203
TELEPHONE: (518) 472-2972
DIRECTOR: Frank G. Carrino
Integral unit of State University of New York at Albany
SUPPORT: parent institution, 100%
PURPOSE: to prepare candidates for teaching careers in history and
   Spanish, diplomatic corps, work abroad with private educational
   and business concerns, and research in the inter-American field
RESEARCH FIELDS: literature, inter-American politics, history,
   sociology, and socioeconomic conditions of Latin America
RESEARCH STAFF: 7 professionals
                3 others
The Center's library is part of the University library:
      16,000 + volumes
      (volume figure includes books, pamphlets, and documents)
      240 + current periodicals
      7 daily newspapers
Library restricted to faculty, staff, and students of the University.

119   *North Carolina. University. Institute of Latin
      American Studies*
FOUNDED: 1940
ADDRESS: P.O. Drawer 110
         Chapel Hill, N.C.
TELEPHONE: (919) 933-1000
DIRECTOR: Frederico G. Gil
Integral unit of the University of North Carolina
SUPPORT: parent institution, 100%
PURPOSE: to conduct research on Latin America, to train students in
   Latin American affairs and culture, and to coordinate publication
   and cooperation with Latin American scholars
RESEARCH FIELDS: economics, history, and political science. Serves as
   a peace corps training center. Areas of concentration are South
   American republics in general

PUBLICATIONS: occasional studies and reports; joint publisher of *Anales* with Facultad Latinoamericana de Ciencias Sociales of Santiago, Chile
RESEARCH STAFF: 12 professionals
              5 others
Maintains a small reading room and reference collection of library materials.

120 *Oregon. University. Institute of International Studies and Overseas Administration*
FOUNDED: 1958
ADDRESS: Eugene, Ore. 97403
TELEPHONE: (503) 342-1411, ext. 1351
DIRECTOR: John Gange
Integral unit of the University of Oregon
SUPPORT: parent institution, 90%; foundations, grants, etc., 10%
PURPOSE: to develop programs of research, teaching, and administration for the developing areas of the world. Cooperates with private and governmental agencies on international programs of exchange and research
RESEARCH FIELDS: social sciences, particularly education, and international relations. All aspects of administration, private and public, and management, including development administration and planning, are stressed
PROPORTION OF RESEARCH ON LATIN AMERICA: 40%
PUBLICATIONS: occasional bulletins and reports (irregular)
RESEARCH STAFF: 3 professionals
              3 supporting professionals
              4 others
LATIN AMERICAN RESEARCH SPECIALISTS: 2.

121 *Pennsylvania. University. Foreign Policy Research Institute*
FOUNDED: 1955
ADDRESS: 133 South 36th St.
        Philadelphia, Pa. 19104
TELEPHONE: (215) EV 2-0685

DIRECTOR: Robert Strausz-Hupe
Separately incorporated unit affiliated with the University of
    Pennsylvania
SUPPORT: University of Pennsylvania, 80%; other funds, 20%
PURPOSE: to conduct research and study on nationalism, Communist
    strategy, military strategy, diplomacy, and international relations
RESEARCH FIELDS: nationalism, communism, arms control and dis-
    armament, inter-American relations, and military strategy
PROPORTION OF RESEARCH ON LATIN AMERICA: 35%
RESEARCH STAFF: 7 professionals
                10 (part-time) supporting professionals
                6 others
LATIN AMERICAN RESEARCH SPECIALISTS: 5.

122   *Puerto Rico. University. Institute of Caribbean Studies*

FOUNDED: 1958
ADDRESS: Río Piedras, P.R. 00926
TELEPHONE: 766-2220
DIRECTOR: Thomas G. Mathews
Integral unit of the University of Puerto Rico's Faculty of Social
    Sciences
SUPPORT: parent institution, 70%; Ford Foundation, 30%
PURPOSE: to stimulate and coordinate research and studies on the
    Caribbean area; to give disciplinary training to the Caribbean
    specialist; and to maintain a publication program for accom-
    plished research
RESEARCH FIELDS: social sciences, particularly interdisciplinary re-
    search such as socioeconomic conditions, history, education, politi-
    cal behavior, and social anthropology for the Caribbean and
    surrounding areas of Latin America
RESEARCH STAFF: 4 professionals
                2 others
PUBLICATIONS: *Caribbean Studies* (quarterly)
                Monographic series (irregular)
                Special studies (irregular)
                Caribbean Monthly Bulletin

Maintains a small collection of library materials:
   2,000 + books, documents, and journals
   12 + newspapers
Stresses the social sciences and humanities for the Caribbean area
Library use restricted to research staff and qualified individuals.
   Interlibrary loan.†

123 *Rutgers University. Institute of Latin American
      Studies*
FOUNDED: 1967
ADDRESS: New Brunswick, N.J. 08903
TELEPHONE: (201) 247-1766
DIRECTOR: Frank Dauster
Recently established integral unit of Rutgers University. Will stress
   research in the social sciences and the humanities, with initial
   projects on Latin American culture, especially that of South
   America.

124 *Southern Illinois University. Latin American
      Institute*
FOUNDED: 1958
ADDRESS: 202 E. Pearl St.
         Carbondale, Ill. 62903
TELEPHONE: (618) 453-2594
DIRECTOR: Albert W. Bork
Integral unit of Southern Illinois University, cooperating with the
   University Museum's Meso-American Cooperative Research
   Program
SUPPORT: parent institution, 70%; U.S. government and other
   research grants, 30%
PURPOSE: to provide a special course of study for students interested
   in Latin America and inter-American studies; to conduct research
   on Latin American culture, anthropology, and history
RESEARCH FIELDS: social sciences, with emphasis on anthropology,
   history, cultural anthropology, and sociology; particularly inter-
   ested in Middle America
RESEARCH STAFF: 4 professionals
               6 others.

125 *Southern Illinois University. University Museum.*
   Meso-American Cooperative Research Program
FOUNDED: 1960
ADDRESS: University Museum, Southern Illinois University
         Carbondale, Ill. 62903
TELEPHONE: (618) 453-2693
DIRECTOR: J. Charles Kelley
Integral unit of the University Museum of Southern Illinois
   University
SUPPORT: parent institution, 90%; other sources, 10%
PURPOSE: to conduct general research in cultural history, cultural
   dynamics, cultural ecology, and cultural anthropology of Meso-
   America, especially northern MesoAmerica
RESEARCH FIELDS: anthropology, archaeology, ethnography, and
   cultural ecology
RESEARCH STAFF: 5 professionals
               8 others.

126 *Stanford Research Institute. International*
   Development Center
FOUNDED: Institute, 1946; Center, 1950
ADDRESS: 333 Ravenswood Ave.
         Menlo Park, Calif. 94025
TELEPHONE: (415) 326-6200, ext. 4339 and 2205
DIRECTOR: Dr. Karl Folkers, President
ADMINISTRATOR, IDC: Wilson F. Harwood
Integral unit of Stanford Research Institute
SUPPORT: U.S. government contracts, 77%; international contracts,
   18%; other, 5%
PURPOSE: SRI is a nonprofit organization performing contract re-
   search for industry, government, and foundations in the United
   States and abroad
RESEARCH FIELDS: economics, education planning, tourism, transpor-
   tation economics, food sciences, industrial development, economic
   planning, business, and regional development
PROPORTION OF RESEARCH ON LATIN AMERICA: 5% (approximately)
RESEARCH STAFF: 1,500 professionals
               1,500 others

LATIN AMERICAN RESEARCH SPECIALISTS: 100
Maintains a special library:
LIBRARIAN: Lorraine Pratt
  28,000 + volumes
  2,000 + current periodicals
  80,000 + documents
  6,000 + pamphlets
  5 newspapers
Library open to the public. No interlibrary loan.

127 *Stanford University. Committee on Latin American Studies*

FOUNDED: 1965
ADDRESS: Bolivar House, Stanford University
      Stanford, Calif. 94305
TELEPHONE: (415) 321-2300, ext. 4444
DIRECTOR: John J. Johnson, Chairman
Integral unit of Stanford University
SUPPORT: parent institution and research grants secured by
  individuals
PURPOSE: Committee is responsible for the planning and coordina-
  tion of Stanford's Latin American program. As an interdepart-
  mental subcommittee of the International Studies Committee, the
  Committee disseminates information on courses, faculty, and
  activities of Latin American interest; directs the M.A. program in
  Latin American Studies; and promotes communication among
  faculty and graduate students of Stanford and neighboring
  universities
RESEARCH FIELDS: social sciences, especially anthropology, business,
  geography, history and political science, development education,
  communications, food research, and Spanish and Portuguese languages and literature
RESEARCH STAFF: permanent staff director and two office assistants.
  All other appointees serve on a visiting basis from several social
  science departments.

128 *Syracuse University. Center for Overseas Operations and Research*

FOUNDED: 1960

ADDRESS: 211 Maxwell Hall
          Syracuse, N.Y. 13203
TELEPHONE: (315) 476-5571, ext. 2106
DIRECTOR: Irving Swerdlow
Integral unit of Maxwell School of Citizenship and Public Affairs
SUPPORT: parent institution
PURPOSE: to perform research on public affairs and development
   administration, international relations, and technical assistance
RESEARCH FIELDS: political studies, development administration,
   public administration, economic development, international rela-
   tions, technical assistance programs, and foreign aid
PROPORTION OF RESEARCH ON LATIN AMERICA: 35%
RESEARCH STAFF: 22 professionals
               17 others
LATIN AMERICAN RESEARCH SPECIALISTS: 8.

129   *Texas. University. Institute of Latin American Studies*

FOUNDED: 1940
ADDRESS: University of Texas
          Austin, Tex. 78712
TELEPHONE: (512) GR 1-5551
DIRECTOR: John P. Harrison
Integral unit of the University of Texas
SUPPORT: parent institution, 65%; grants and contracts, 35%
PURPOSE: coordinates research and academic work relating to Latin
   America; also grants undergraduate and graduate degrees
RESEARCH FIELDS: Central American demography, business, anthro-
   pology, and sociology; also South American history and anthro-
   pology. 75% of all research is devoted to Central America
RESEARCH STAFF: 4 professionals
               16 others
PUBLICATIONS: *Latin American Research Review*
               occasional reports and publications
The Latin American collection is part of the main library holdings
   at the University of Texas (see entry 65).

130   *Tulane University. Middle American Research Institute*

FOUNDED: 1924
ADDRESS: New Orleans, La. 70118
TELEPHONE: (504) 865-7711, ext. 238
DIRECTOR: Robert Wauchope
Integral unit of Tulane University
SUPPORT: parent institution and grants from outside sources;
   percentages vary from year to year
PURPOSE: to conduct research and publication programs in the
   humanities and social sciences on Mexico and Central America
RESEARCH FIELDS: humanities and social sciences, with emphasis on
   anthropology, economics, history, and sociology. Mexico and
   Central American republics are stressed, especially Nicaragua and
   Costa Rica
RESEARCH STAFF: 12 professionals
                 5 others
PUBLICATIONS: *Publications of the Middle American Research*
              Institute
              Handbook of Middle American Indians
              miscellaneous research reports and monographs
The Latin American Library for the Middle American Research
   Institute is part of the main library. For information concerning
   this collection, see entry 67.

131   *Tulane University. Middle American Research Insti-*
       tute. Inter-American Institute for Musical Research
FOUNDED: 1961
ADDRESS: New Orleans, La. 70118
TELEPHONE: (504) 865-7711
DIRECTOR: Gilbert Chase
Integral unit of the Middle American Research Institute
SUPPORT: parent institution and grants from outside sources; per-
   centages of support fluctuate from year to year
PURPOSE: to conduct a research and publication program on the
   musical arts and history of the Americas
RESEARCH FIELDS: musical arts, musicology, history of music and
   folk music of the Americas, particularly for Mexico and Central
   America
RESEARCH STAFF: 2 professionals
                2 others

PUBLICATIONS: *Yearbook of Inter-American Musicology*

Maintains a cataloged and classified archive of materials for the study of music in the Americas that includes scores, manuscripts, tapes, disc recordings, books, periodicals, microfilms, and documents of every kind. Total number of items in this collection exceeds 10,000.

132 *United States. Library of Congress. Hispanic Foundation*

FOUNDED: 1939

ADDRESS: Library of Congress
 Washington, D.C. 20540

TELEPHONE: (202) 426-5400

DIRECTOR: Howard F. Cline

ASST. DIRECTOR: Donald F. Wisdom

Integral unit of the Library of Congress

SUPPORT: federal government, 100%

PURPOSE: to maintain a special reference collection of works dealing with Hispanic culture and to assist researchers using the Library of Congress's collections. The continuing responsibilities include specialized reference service, bibliographical enterprises, and the recommendation of acquisitions for purchase, exchange, and gifts of suitable materials for the general collections of the library in all fields with a Hispanic interest

RESEARCH FIELDS: all of Latin America and most subjects

RESEARCH STAFF: 9 professionals
 8 others

PUBLICATIONS: *Handbook of Latin American Studies* (annual)
 occasional monographs

Maintains a small reference and working collection, relying mainly on the various collections in the Library of Congress.

133 *Vanderbilt University. Graduate Center for Latin American Studies*

FOUNDED: 1961

ADDRESS: Nashville, Tenn. 37203

TELEPHONE: (615) 254-5411, ext. 6482

DIRECTOR: Eric N. Baklanoff

Integral unit of Vanderbilt University
SUPPORT: parent institution, 60%; federal government, 25%;
  foundations, 15%
PURPOSE: to conduct research and studies on Latin America
RESEARCH FIELDS: anthropology, business, economics, geography, history, literature, political science, and sociology. Brazil, Chile, and Colombia are countries of particular interest
RESEARCH STAFF: 4 professionals
              2 others
PUBLICATIONS: occasional papers
Maintains a small library on Latin America
BIBLIOGRAPHER AND CATALOGER: James Montgomery.

134   *Wisconsin. University. Center for International*
      Business Research
FOUNDED: 1965
ADDRESS: Commerce Building
        Madison, Wis. 53706
TELEPHONE: (608) 262-4351
DIRECTOR: William Glade
Integral unit of the University of Wisconsin
SUPPORT: parent institution, 70%; Ford Foundation, 30%
PURPOSE: to encourage faculty research on the subject of Latin American business and industrial development, and to assist in the training of graduate students for this area of research
RESEARCH FIELDS: national market development, transportation policies and problems, industrial development, and labor relations
RESEARCH STAFF: 7 professionals
              11 others.

135   *Wisconsin. University. Language and Area Center*
      for Latin American Studies
FOUNDED: 1930
ADDRESS: 267 Social Sciences Building
        Madison, Wis. 53706
TELEPHONE: (608) 262-2811
DIRECTOR: Norman P. Sacks
Integral unit of the University of Wisconsin

SUPPORT: parent institution, 60%; federal government, 15%; Ford
   Foundation, 25%
PURPOSE: to encourage and coordinate research and publication on
   Latin America by faculty and students
RESEARCH FIELDS: Spanish and Portuguese language and linguistics;
   Portuguese and Brazilian literature and civilization. Latin Ameri-
   can countries are investigated in the areas of economics, geog-
   raphy, anthropology, history, agricultural economics, and rural
   sociology
RESEARCH STAFF: 10 professionals
                        5 others
PUBLICATIONS: *Luzo Brazilian Review* (irregular).

ADDENDA

The materials listed as part of the collections for the following institutions were not secured from source, from direct investigations, or from questionnaire survey techniques. Rather, they are from secondary sources and therefore do not carry the full weight of authority and reliability. The sources from which the information on these entries was secured are:

Lee Ash and Denis Lorenz. *Subject collections.* 3d rev. ed. New York: Bowker, 1967.

Anthony T. Kruzas. *Directory of special libraries and information centers.* 2d ed. Detroit: Gale Research, 1968.

1968–1969 American library directory. 26th ed. New York: Bowker, 1968.

136 *California. University. Library*
FOUNDED: 1954
ADDRESS: Riverside, Calif. 92507
TELEPHONE: (714) 787-3223
LIBRARIAN: Donald G. Wilson
Latin American library materials are not quantified, but they are in excess of 17,000 volumes
SPECIAL COLLECTIONS: Argentine politics and Paraguay
SUBJECT STRENGTHS: Argentina, Paraguay, and South America in general, with emphasis on geography, government, and political science.†

137 *Claremont College. Honnold Library*
FOUNDED: joint library dedicated 1952
ADDRESS: 9th and Dartmouth Sts.
         Claremont, Calif. 91711

TELEPHONE: (714) 626-8511, ext. 2215
LIBRARIAN: Richard D. Johnson
SPECIAL COLLECTIONS: Latin America and Mexican newspapers
(19th century)
SUBJECT STRENGTHS: Mexico, with general coverage of Latin America; economics, government, history, literature, and politics
INTERLIBRARY LOAN: yes. Library open to public, but circulation is
restricted to students, staff, and faculty.†

138   Cleveland. Public Library. History, Biography and Travel Department

FOUNDED: 1913
ADDRESS: 325 Superior Ave.
            Cleveland, Ohio 44114
TELEPHONE: (216) 241-1020
LIBRARIAN: Donna L. Root
SPECIAL COLLECTION: Latin American Room (research sources)
SUBJECT STRENGTHS: archaeology, current affairs, geography, history,
exploration and travel, and political affairs
    16,000 volumes
    30 serials
    5,000 brochures and maps
    Miscellaneous documents and ephemeral materials
INTERLIBRARY LOAN: yes. Open to public.†

139   Knox College. H. M. Seymour Library

FOUNDED: 1841
ADDRESS: Galesburg, Ill. 61401
TELEPHONE: (309) 343-1121, ext. 246 and 346
LIBRARIAN: Warren Morris
SUBJECT STRENGTHS: economics and history of Latin America
    15,000 volumes
    Other materials not quantified
INTERLIBRARY LOAN: yes. Library open to public on a restricted
basis.†

140   *New York. State University. Hawley Library*
FOUNDED: 1848
ADDRESS: 135 Western Ave.
             Albany, N.Y. 12203
TELEPHONE: (518) 457-8542
LIBRARIAN: Daniel A. Newberry, Humanities bibliographer
SPECIAL COLLECTION: Mexican education
SUBJECT STRENGTHS: contemporary Latin American poetry, fiction,
    and drama; Latin American government and economics
        5,000 volumes
        100 serials
INTERLIBRARY LOAN: yes. Library open to public for reference use
    only.†

141   *San Diego State College. Library*
FOUNDED: 1897
ADDRESS: San Diego, Calif. 92115
TELEPHONE: (714) 286-6014
LIBRARIAN: Louis A. Kenney
SUBJECT STRENGTHS: education, economics, history, political science,
    and public affairs. Mexico is well represented
        22,000 volumes
INTERLIBRARY LOAN: yes. Library open to public, but circulation is
    restricted to students, staff, and faculty.†

142   *United States. School of the Americas. Biblioteca
        de las Américas*
FOUNDED: 1961
ADDRESS: Building 400
             Fort Gulick, Canal Zone
TELEPHONE: Fort Gulick, 2753
LIBRARIAN: Shirley B. Welshinger
SPECIAL COLLECTION: guerrilla and jungle warfare
SUBJECT STRENGTHS: foreign relations, full coverage of Latin America
    (including fiction), military science, and military history
        8,000 volumes
        120 serials

31 Vertical File drawers of pamphlets
13 newspapers
INTERLIBRARY LOAN: yes. Library use is restricted.

143   *University of the Pacific. Library*
FOUNDED: 1851
ADDRESS: Stockton, Calif. 95204

TELEPHONE: (209) 466-4841
LIBRARIAN: James A. Riddles
LATIN AMERICAN LIBRARY SPECIALIST: James M. Perrin
SPECIAL COLLECTION: Colección Presidente López Mateos
    (3,000 items)
SUBJECT STRENGTHS: Mexican government and history and Latin
    America in general
    7,000 volumes
    Miscellaneous maps, manuscripts, and documents not presently
    quantified
INTERLIBRARY LOAN: yes. Library open to public on a restricted
    basis.†

144   *Wisconsin. University. Agricultural Economics Library*
FOUNDED: 1927
ADDRESS: Room 301, Hiram Hall
          Madison, Wis. 53706
TELEPHONE: (608) 262-3520
LIBRARIAN: Patricia Peterson
SPECIAL COLLECTION: Land Tenure Center collection
SUBJECT STRENGTHS: economics and land tenure reform in
    Latin America
    1,500 volumes
    Unquantified number of maps and pictures
    10 5-drawer file cabinets
Library use restricted.

INDEXES

COUNTRY AND REGIONAL INDEX

The inclusion of a library or research center within this index is necessarily based upon three conditions: (1) the institution is conducting extensive research and/or training programs devoted specifically to that Latin American country or region; (2) a library through its acquisition program is responsible for securing all publications issued from a particular country or region, such as under the Farmington Plan, or; (3) a library in support of a teaching and/or research program, or in the maintenance and development of a special collection, secures all pertinent print and nonprint items by or about a particular country or region in Latin America. The inclusion of a library or research center in this section, therefore, is based upon information provided by the institutions themselves, without an extensive evaluation of quantitative or qualitative data.

Numbers listed refer to entries, not to pages.

LATIN AMERICAN LIBRARY SPECIALISTS

Numbers listed refer to entries, not to pages.

SUBJECT INDEX

Numbers listed refer to entries, not to pages.